Dedication

To the Incomparable One
Whose
mighty acts and
glorious interventions
are recounted
throughout
the pages
of this
book.

Quiet Miracles

And Other True Stories of God's Guidance, Provision and Care

Charles W. Shepson

May the Lord wonderfully bless and use you!

Charles Shepson

Colleen's husband

see pp 248 and following...

Christian Publications

CAMP HILL, PENNSYLVANIA

⌐◻⌐īChristian Publications

3825 Hartzdale Drive, Camp Hill, PA 17011
www.cpi-horizon.com
www.christianpublications.com

Faithful, biblical publishing since 1883

Quiet Miracles
ISBN: 0-87509-885-1
LOC Control Number: 01-131621

© 2001 Christian Publications, Inc.
All rights reserved
Printed in the United States of America

01   02   03   04   05   5   4   3   2

Contents

1956-1958

1961-1970

1972-1979

1995-1996

Foreword

*T*heory can be very helpful but when it comes to discussing God's working in the lives of His children, it is difficult to beat personal experience. I have known Charles Shepson for over half a century as a student, a colleague, and especially as a friend. Through those years I have seen God working in his life with what he describes in this book as "quiet miracles."

My first contact with the author came when I was visiting the Cranford Alliance Church in New Jersey. I sat in on a meeting of the young people and was very impressed with the poise and abilities of the young high school student serving as its president. His name was Charles Shepson. Later he enrolled at what is now Nyack College and applied for student employment in the college book store which I was then managing. He proved to be one of my most efficient employees and our friendship developed. After graduating with a diploma and taking a pastorate, he returned to complete his degree. I found him an outstanding student in the class he took with me. God has gifted him with a unique ability to communicate not only in the pulpit but also in the classroom and in conference ministries. We served together for nearly a decade at what is now Crown College, and over and over again I would see how God used him in working with, teaching, and counseling students. Student deans find great difficulty in combining the pastoral role and the role of the disciplinarian and rule enforcer! Charles had the unusual ability to combine both well, and even in those sad instances when a student's behavior caused him to have to leave the college, the student could not miss the concern and pastoral care of his dean. When God called him back into the pastorate about fifty miles from the college, I had many opportunities to get acquainted with his congregation during the various times he would invite me to minister. I learned not only of their love for their pastor but also of the many ways God was working through him in strengthening their faith with the "quiet miracles" they saw God working in their midst.

We later talked together about the vision God had given him for a ministry that would provide a place for hurting Christian workers to come for healing. This would also be a quiet place for those who needed somewhere to retreat when the pressures of Christian ministry became so great that a special time with God was a necessity. Fairhaven Ministries was to be its name. I had the joy of being on its first Board of Reference and have also served for several years more recently as a member of its Board of Directors. Over and over again in that ministry we have shared in those "quiet miracles" that God has performed in using Fairhaven as the place where so many Christian workers have been refreshed.

This book has been written in such a way that much of it becomes an autobiography. That is not a weakness but a strength, for it encourages us to recognize that God's interest in us is not just now and then but is an on-going commitment of Divine love to His children. Our own trust in God can be encouraged and strengthened as we read the pages of this book and see how, over and over again, the hand of God has been evidenced in the way He has watched over His servant throughout his life. Through joys, through heartaches, through the daily pressures of living, the author has found the mercy of the Lord has consistently been present, and this book reminds us that "by His mighty power at work within us, He is able to accomplish infinitely more than we would ever dare to ask or hope (Ephesians 3:20, NLT)." *Quiet Miracles* is the story of God's working in and through the life of Charles Shepson.

Donald J. Trouten

Preface

I promised myself that I would someday write a book on the subject of "The Silence of God." I had heard too many people ask the questions "Why is God silent?" and "Why does He not speak aloud today?"

My contention is that God does speak . . . *frequently*.

I agree with Elihu when he insists, "God *does* speak—now one way, now another—though man may not perceive it" (Job 33:14, emphasis added). Our problem is that most of those times His voice is a "gentle whisper" (1 Kings 19:12), and we are simply too busy and noisy and earthbound in our interests to hear those extra-soft, "*gentle*" whispers! "[H]ow *faint* the whisper we hear of him!" (Job 26:14, emphasis added).

When I had completed this manuscript, originally penned for my grandchildren, it suddenly dawned upon me that I had just finished a book stating forcefully that God certainly is *not* silent. In fact, sometimes His voice is very loud, clear and emphatic! ". . . he *thunders* with his majestic voice"(37:4, emphasis added).

My prayer is that you will hear Him speaking loudly and clearly as you read, *and* that you will determine to listen continually for His thrilling voice to your own heart in the days to come, whether He chooses to shout or to whisper very, *very* softly.

This book was first published under the title, *To Stephanie and Steven, with Love, from Grampa*. It was Anthony Bollback who gave me the idea (or was it God, through him?). When I wrote to commend him for authoring *To China and Back* (number four in the Jaffray Series of missionary biographies), he told me that when he was approached about submitting a manuscript describing his missionary experiences, he was thrilled. *He had already written it!* It had been the result of a desire to record for his grandchildren the marvelous workings of the Lord that he had experienced. When he wrote those chapters, he never dreamed that one day thousands would read what he had written for a few.

I had never considered writing an entire book for only two people, but I was intrigued by the idea. I decided to follow his example. I wrote the book in the hopes that our grandchildren would see the reality of God in their grandparents' real-life experiences, and would pray the same prayer I prayed sitting in front of the fireplace that night in South Bound Brook, New Jersey.

But wait! I'm getting ahead of myself and slipping into chapter 2 prematurely. Please read this book thoughtfully. Let God clearly speak to your heart, challenging you to follow Him completely. He is unquestionably worthy of your complete trust and unswerving allegiance.

1934 -1946

Who gave man his mouth? Who makes him deaf
or mute? Who gives him sight or makes him
blind? Is it not I, the LORD?
(Exodus 4:11)

God's Cornucopia

1934

I don't remember a lot about my childhood. There are some things I have tried to forget, in fact. We were *very* poor, though I was not really aware of it at the time.

One Thanksgiving Eve my mother opened the cupboards in that little kitchen in South Bound Brook, New Jersey, and found only one box of lentils. There was nothing else. The Great Depression had cost my dad his job, and then his almost-paid-for, spacious home. We had moved into a ramshackle duplex, rent-free, with the stipulation that my father work on the dilapidated old place to improve it, in lieu of paying rent. Mrs. Cassard, the owner, had a lot of rental units and she took pity on us as we had no place to find shelter.

"Well," my mother said with a heavy sigh, "we'll just have lentil soup for Thanksgiving."

But she was not thinking about our loving God who cares so deeply for us.

Though I was only six years old, I can still remember clearly the knock that came at the front door and what it brought! The man had in his arms two big bags of groceries from the local Lions Club. How we rejoiced as we unpacked a ham, cans of beans and vegetables, celery, cheese, nuts and assorted other things. The old Kalamazoo stove (that would bring a fortune now as an antique) had no fire in it yet, so Mom arranged those things on the cold, highly polished surface of the stove.

Scarcely had the last item been unpacked when we heard someone cautiously climbing the creaky steps to the back porch. We hurried out and found one of the members of the Dutch Reformed Church at our back door. He said that they had prepared grocery baskets for some of the people in our town who were going through difficult times. They knew my dad had been laid off at the railroad, so they had packed a big one for us.

With great excitement we began unloading that basket. It had a huge turkey in it as well as potatoes, lettuce, radishes, yams, cans of soup, cranberry jelly and pumpkin for making a pie. There were so many other things, it was difficult to fit them all on the stove top.

But that was not the end of that never-to-be-forgotten evening! A few minutes later there was someone at the front door again. It was a man from the Kiwanis Club. He had a box in which we found two chickens, and all the trimmings for a wonderful Thanksgiving dinner.

Lentil soup? *Not this Thanksgiving!* God had opened His own cornucopia of blessing and poured out so much that there was not room enough for it on the stove; we had to use the kitchen table, too.

Each Generation Must Refight the Crucial Battles

1938

*P*astor Charles Downs probably considered it a routine call on a family in his church. For me, it was far more. As I sat in our little living room there in South Bound Brook, New Jersey, listening to my parents and our pastor reminisce, I was deeply impressed. They were talking about the early days of The Christian and Missionary Alliance. To a ten-year-old boy, Old Orchard Beach, Maine and the full-bearded Dr. A.B. Simpson who held conventions there seemed as far away as the legendary David Livingstone in Africa (well, *almost*). But Simpson came alive as they reflected upon stirring missionary messages so moving that people actually removed pieces of jewelry and put them in the offering plate. His hearers eagerly wanted to help send the good news to the lost and in that way hasten the return of the Lord Jesus. They told of fantastic physical healings that took place as this Presbyterian minister, who had himself been marvelously healed of a severe heart condition, taught divine healing. The accounts of the miracles, the missionary movement and the reckless abandon of sincere believers made a profound impression upon my young heart.

After Pastor Downs had read from the Scriptures and had prayed, he left our home. My parents prepared to go up to bed.

"Mom," I said, "may I stay here by the fire for awhile?"

My mother made a quick judgment. "All right, but don't stay up too long; tomorrow is a school day, you know," she said.

I curled up on the couch and stared into the glowing embers, watching an occasional spark zigzag up into the chimney. I was in a very pensive mood. I remembered God's bountiful provision on that Thanksgiving Eve four years earlier, but to a ten-year-old that seemed like a very long time ago. "Lord Jesus," I prayed, "I am not content to hear about miracles performed in the good old days; I want to experience Your power in my life and generation. Please let me see for myself how real You are, and what powerful things You can do."

I never dreamed that night how beautifully and fully God would answer that sincere prayer from a little boy's heart. The rest of this book will be the unfolding of the answer to that prayer.

John Gardner had not yet penned these words that he would later publish in his book *Self Renewal*: "Each generation must refight the crucial battles and either bring new vitality to its beliefs or else they will die away." By the dying fire that night the refighting of the crucial battles began for me. We all must learn to "refight the crucial battles," so that our faith may become vital and vibrant like the faith of our godly forefathers.

Doctors! Doctors! Doctors!

1938

*S*piritually, I was growing in the Lord. I was a sincere boy with a strong desire to know God better. Physically, I was not doing well at all, and nobody seemed to know why.

I was having fainting spells sometimes, and near-fainting spells with increasing frequency. I would fall unconscious on my way to school, lie there briefly and then regain my consciousness, pick up my scattered books, brush off my clothes and go on to school.

Sometimes that loss of consciousness happened in school as I sat at my desk. When I made a sudden twist to see something at the side of me, sometimes I blacked out and fell off my chair into the aisle, badly frightening my teacher and my classmates. Usually I would quickly regain consciousness and promptly get up off the floor.

I had pains in different parts of my body unpredictably. Sometimes, without being able to give a reason I would start to cry. I felt like crying, so I just cried and cried. My parents were at their wits' end. One doctor after another could find nothing wrong with me physically.

Finally one of the doctors advised them to take me to a child psychiatrist. He suspected that there might be nothing wrong with me at all. All those pains, the fainting spells and the crying were almost certainly psychological in nature, he insisted.

Dr. Dagenhart gave me a thorough examination. Then, finding nothing wrong, he began to talk to me like this. "Hold your thumb out in front of you. Now, think about that thumb. Imagine it is hurting you. The pain is getting worse and worse. Do you feel that terrible pain?"

"No," I answered truthfully.

"Just keep thinking about that thumb and the throbbing pain in it," he persisted. "It is beginning to hurt now, isn't it?"

I could see that he rather badly wanted me to say "Yes" to him, so I lied a little. "Well, maybe it hurts some," I said.

He kept coaxing me, and finally because I was tired of it all, and not wanting to keep disappointing the man, I agreed that it was beginning to hurt me a lot now. I could tell he was pleased! He had what he wanted.

He met with my parents and told them that my pains and all the other symptoms were merely psychosomatic. They were all manufactured in my mind and were not real. I was what they termed a "hypochondriac." My symptoms had no physiological origin, he insisted. They were all imagined!

I knew that was not true. So did my mother.

Meanwhile I kept getting worse and worse. I cannot tell you how many different doctors my parents took me to for further examinations. I think I was seen by more than three dozen doctors.

Then one day while we were in a department store, a clerk was not watching where he was going, and the clothing bin on wheels that he was pushing ran into me. It barely grazed my heel. All I needed was a Band-Aid, but he took me to the first aid room where the store nurse cleansed it with alcohol (ouch!) and then bandaged it rather impressively. I objected! A simple little Band-Aid would have been enough.

Very shortly after that incident a man representing the store came to our home. He had release papers he wanted me to sign, stating that I had not been seriously injured. For signing that he offered me a $100 check! That was a lot of money in 1938. He also said that he wanted me to go to any doctor my parents chose. The doctor was to look at my heel and sign papers stating that the injury was minor.

We went to see a general practitioner in Bound Brook, New Jersey. "As long as the insurance company is paying for this," the doctor said, "why don't I give you a thorough physical." He did a *very* thorough one, in fact. When he tried to get reflex actions from my knees, to his surprise there were none. He knocked gently on them with his rubber mallet as I dangled the lower half of my legs off the edge of the cold examination table. He tried and tried. There were no reflexive responses to be found. That led him to a very careful examination of my spine. Even without x-rays, he came to the conclusion that I had been born with a defective spine. He noticed when I stood that one shoulder was lower than the other. He measured the girth of my legs and discovered one was significantly smaller in girth than the other. He was on to something, and he knew it!

God used that general practitioner to uncover my *real* problems, leading to referral to orthopedic and neuro-surgeons who quickly recognized the spina bifida condition. We were on the right track, but the kinds of things they talked about in the way of sophisticated and complicated operations were way beyond what my parents could afford. *I might not get treatment*, I thought, *but at least I no longer have to be embarrassed about the psychiatrist saying it is all in my head!*

God says our steps are ordered by the Lord. So, when I stepped in front of that clothing cart and got that little nick on my heel, God's angels were guiding me, even into the pathway of pain, for my ultimate good. There would be many more doctors, but at least these would know what the problem was, and perhaps God would use one of them to help me.

God's Answer to a Big Problem

1939

*T*here was no way my parents could afford the kind of orthopedic surgery some of the doctors were suggesting. Anyway, the doctors seemed uncertain of themselves as to the diagnosis and even as to the prognosis if the surgery route were followed. One orthopedic surgeon wanted to operate on my spine and then have me lie on a wide board for six months completely immobile. Another was certain that was the wrong approach to take. Funds were not available for such surgery anyway.

One day there came a knock at our front door. There stood one of the tallest, most distinguished-looking men I had ever seen. He was *very* well dressed. He asked if he might come in. He introduced himself as Mr. Hutchinson. I later discovered that he lived in a mansion up on the side of the mountain overlooking our town. Mr. Hutchinson said that he had heard of my crippled condition. He told my parents that he was with an organization that helped finance hospitals for crippled children all across the country, and that they did all their work absolutely free! He asked if he might be given permission to "sponsor" me. That involved his taking some pictures of the distortion of my body, as well as his sending in a form nominating me to be one of the children they would receive. My folks gave him permission.

I was admitted to the Hospital for Crippled Children on Roosevelt Avenue in Philadelphia, Pennsylvania. During the next year I received not only excellent care, but also an experimental operation involving a number of orthopedic surgeons and neurosurgeons. They rebuilt my spine, using an eleven inch slab of bone from my good leg to repair the numerous vertebrae in my spine that had been incompletely formed in the womb. They told my parents that I would probably never walk again, but that my life would be spared by this surgery. Without it, they warned, it was only a matter of time until a fall would end my life suddenly or at the very least leave me a paraplegic. In total, I received thousands of dollars worth of repair work on my body in a day when bread was ten cents a loaf, a Pepsi Cola was only a nickel and a haircut cost twenty-five cents.

Though *we* had very little financially, *God* has never been poor, except when He laid aside His wealth and came to earth to live as a child in the home of poor parents. God has His answers to every problem, no matter how big the need may be. Through a man we had never seen before, God brought to us the offer of not only thousands of dollars worth of medical treatment, but also the services and skill of the finest orthopedic surgeon in the country at that time, Dr. John Royal Moore. Dr. Moore is to this day something of a legend in orthopedic history, and I had the privilege of being one of the benefactors of his charitable services to the children who were admitted to this specialized hospital in Philadelphia.

A "Different" Private Nurse

1940

*L*et me back up a little here. The experimental surgery Dr. John Royal Moore and his seven colleagues proposed was risky and uncertain. He was a man of few words. Those words erupted abruptly from his mouth in staccato sounds, like bullets from an automatic weapon. He sat behind his desk, wearing dark glasses, and quickly spelled out the prognosis.

"We don't know whether your son will come off the operating table alive or not. We are quite certain he will never walk again, but if my plan works, this will spare his life. Otherwise he could die at any time. With the surgery, he might be able to live and develop in many ways. I am willing to do this along with three other orthopedic surgeons and four neurosurgeons. We will do our combined best to complete his spine with bone from his leg if you wish us to try. You will have to take care of him for life, if he ends up paralyzed or incapacitated in any way. If you simply wish to let nature take its course, we certainly will understand. The decision is yours."

The answer my mother gave was immediate: "You go ahead and do the things you can, Dr. Moore. We believe in divine healing. God will do the things you cannot."

I was still in one of those glass cubicles they put the newcomers in to "decontaminate" them. The theory was that after three weeks in isolation, the children could no longer come down with any of the communicable childhood diseases, for they would not have had exposure to them during those twenty-one days. They could not risk placing us in with the other children, for there were casts to be seen everywhere in that big ward where twenty-four children lay in beds, row upon row, all having orthopedic problems. I had "served my time" now, but there was no room to move me out with the other children.

For three weeks the doctors and nurses had double-gowned and double-masked themselves when they came in to take care of me. I was all alone in that small glass hospital room. I dreaded surgery and its aftermath with no one to stay with me. Parents were not allowed inside the hospital. Nurses were in very short supply. *Would I have the proper postoperative care?* I wondered, since there were no private nurses and no recovery room.

In the cubicle next to mine was a boy about my own age. We conversed by writing notes and holding them up to the glass. I learned his name was Elvin Ingham, from Altoona, Pennsylvania.

One day he held up an opened New Testament. He pressed it against the glass and pointed to an underlined verse. I was thrilled. *Perhaps he was a Christian!*

Our friendship developed rapidly, even though we had to resort to hand gestures, charades and written notes or passages from our Bibles pressed against the window in order to share them with one another.

Shortly before my surgery, the head nurse came around. We were all afraid of her. Her square jaw and thin lips firmly set gave the impression of her being a brusque sergeant or something worse. She had an impressive black stripe on her stiffly starched nurse's cap, the shape of which made her look half-nun, half-nurse. Often she crossed her muscular arms and stared at her petrified patients with her dark, piercing eyes. She was infamous among us "inmates" for being a strict, no-nonsense, heartless disciplinarian.

In her crisp, unloving manner and a louder voice than usual, she barked out her instructions. She was trying to make her announcement as few times as possible, hoping it would be heard in more than one room at a time through our left-ajar doors. Her startling news brought excitement to all of us who had been waiting to be taken out into the ward. "We have more patients coming in. We have no room for them in cubicles, so those of you who have been here for more than three weeks will be sharing a cubicle, since you are now fully decontaminated."

My roommate was to be Elvin. *Oh, how I rejoiced!* Elvin's bed was pushed and tugged and squeezed into my cubicle. It was crowded, but I didn't mind. For the first time in four weeks, I had someone to talk to whenever I wanted.

Elvin was very pleasant. He was different. I don't mean odd, just *different*. I have never before nor since met anyone quite like him. He was very serious, and yet enjoyable to be with. He seemed very knowledgeable concerning the Bible, yet he revealed that he had never before had fellowship with another Christian. He told me he had "found" the New Testament. He didn't talk of having been "saved" as I would, but he very obviously knew the Lord rather intimately. He was both delightfully and decidedly *different* from others.

I didn't realize all God had in mind when He had them move Elvin in with me. Not only did we have wonderful fellowship together, but also, following my eight long hours of surgery, when I was wheeled back to my room so terribly sick, Elvin became my private "nurse." For days he fed me every meal. The nurses simply didn't have the time, and I was too sick to care. Without the loving attention of my God-given roommate and "nurse" during those days when my life hung in the balance, I am not certain I would have made it.

I wonder if Elvin is still alive. I wonder if he continued to be faithful in his Christian walk. Somehow I think a serendipity of heaven will be meeting my private "nurse"/friend of those very critical days when my life was in danger. Sometimes I even wonder if I will meet him as a fellow Christian with a place in heaven because of the saving grace of Christ, *or* if I will make a new discovery about him there, one I never dreamed of while I was with him in the Hospital for Crippled Children in Philadelphia.* Maybe he never returned to Altoona when we parted. Just maybe he went back to where he had *really* come from in the first place!

*Hebrews 1:14

The Day the Band Played On

1940

*T*he *Fourth of July!* Four simple words when viewed alone, but stand them tall, line them up military-style, spit them out rapidly, add a crisp exclamation point and they literally explode in a colorful collage of red, white and blue, complete with sights, sounds and smells! Yet all of that could happen only in a little boy's imagination, unless. . . .

But first come back with me to my very confined existence. Share my spina-bifida-affected June. School was out and children were prancing and bike-riding, hide-and-seeking and skinny-dipping to their hearts content—other children, I mean.

My greatest joy was being released from the Hospital for Crippled Children in Philadelphia. In spite of a body cast from my neck to my knee, they somehow crammed me into the backseat of a car for the long ride to South Bound Brook, New Jersey. What a grotesque procedure the neighbors saw from behind their window curtains. They were fascinated as they watched my parents unloading with grunts and tugs and threats of hernia this pure white, plaster of paris, bomblike blob. A human head and three and one-half human limbs protruded from it. I felt so helpless. I was dead weight, unable to do a single thing to help them.

The side-by-side apartments in which we lived were crouched right at the sidewalk's edge in a claustrophobic neighborhood. Their only redeeming feature was a vacant corner lot adjacent to the side we occupied. We had turned that into a manicured lawn complete with colorful flower beds. The whole neighborhood seemed to appreciate that parklike oasis.

I took up a three-month residence in the first floor dining room in a hospital bed. I can't remember who provided the bed. We could afford nothing!

At first the sheer joy of deliverance from the hospital atmosphere transformed my days into a little bit of heaven. No more immodest hospital gowns (even little boys have some modesty). No more monotonous institutional food. No more humiliation of asking for a bedpan or urinal from an overworked stranger.

But then boredom set in. Four walls, a ceiling with 108 tiles, one window (but not close enough for much of a glimpse of the outside world), a giant cast iron register for a coal-burning furnace in the center of the floor (I could see it when they rolled me over on my side) and a narrow staircase leading to a second-floor bedroom-bathroom area—that was my world.

The family spent a lot of time with me, but on hot summer nights I knew they really wanted to be out on that screened-in back porch where the hand-cranked Motorola record player stood tall and majestic, where the swing was and where an occasional breeze made tolerable the intense heat of the sultry summer.

It was there we could see the town's people come and go from Minnie DeGroot's ice cream parlor licking their summertime "air-conditioners." We had no mechanical ones. Handheld fans and ice cream cones were the best we could muster.

I was ecstatic when Dad built a crude, narrow stretcher on wheels for me! It had to be *very* narrow to negotiate the turns through the kitchen and back hall onto that screened-in porch. As narrow as it was, the trip still had to be executed like a precise war maneuver. First I had to be slid over onto the stretcher while someone held it close to the bed. I couldn't help much. The eleven-inch incision on my one good leg, where they had taken bone out to rebuild my spine was still a bit tender (or so I thought). My arms were weak from disuse.

Next began the exciting bumpy ride through kitchen and laundry room hall and over the raised sill out onto the airy porch. *I loved it.* Wide-eyed, I took in every detail of those rooms: the Kalamazoo wood stove with the warming ovens above, the coal scuttle I used to fill daily before I had become too physically handicapped, the big kitchen table, the narrow hallway. I marveled that we could make it through there. That seemed like a minor miracle in itself.

Oh, how invigorating the fresh air, the sunshine, the blue sky and the outside world were! People stopped by to chat briefly on their way to the corner grocery or Minnie DeGroot's. I loved it, except in the afternoon when the sun got around to shining in on my cast. Sometimes I reluctantly had to ask to be taken back into the confines of that little dining room. It was just too hot out there on the back porch.

Then one day a truck rolled up. Workmen unloaded and installed a large canvas awning. The mayor of the town owned an awning factory. It was his gift to me! I cried. Now I could stay out there all day long, in my much bigger world.

Wednesday evenings were the highlight of the week! The band practiced on the school's playground six blocks from our house. When the wind was right I could almost imagine them playing right in front of me as I closed my eyes tightly and fantasized. I wrote a letter to the bandmaster and told him how much I enjoyed their playing. He read it to the whole band! They played with even more gusto after that to be sure I could hear.

One sultry Wednesday evening when the sound was not reaching me well, I thought I noticed a decided change taking place. The sound of music was getting stronger. No change in the weather was relieving the almost unbearable itching under my cast, yet I felt sure that I could hear the band better. It was nearly time for them to pack up their instruments and go home. I knew their schedule well.

Suddenly, I realized they were coming my way! What a thrill to see them stiffly march into sight, maneuver the corner so precisely and parade right onto our lawn, in front of the awning! I could barely see them through the mist in my eyes. They played one for me, and then crisply turned and marched back to the school. The fading sounds of slightly off-key instruments were so beautiful. I can never remember a band sounding better. From that unforgettable night on through the summer of 1939 my midweek was exciting, for I knew that when they finished their field maneuvers, they would come and play one for me.

When the Fourth of July approached, I read in the newspaper that our small town was planning the biggest parade in its history. There would be marching bands, shiny fire trucks, the impressive new ambulance of which our town was so proud, funny clowns, prancing twirlers, neatly uniformed scout troops and all the kinds of things that make a young boy's eyes grow bigger by the moment.

Did I dare to write another letter? I wondered. Why not? What was there to lose other than the nickel for the stamp?

> Dear Parade Master:
>
> I was reading in the paper about the parade you are planning, and I noticed that the route is passing just one block from my house. Do you think it would be possible to change it just enough so that it would go past my lawn? I would so very much like to see the parade, and not just hear it from a block away!

Their well-kept secret exploded into one of the greatest days of a young boy's life when on that Fourth of July morning, the Parade Master himself showed up on *my* lawn, beneath *my* awning and told me he had a surprise for *me*. The parade would start right there! Every band would first march onto our lawn, play a number for me and then take its place in the lineup.

Wide-eyed and with rapidly beating heart I watched and listened as band after band formed on our lawn, or marched onto it, and with gusto played an ear-splitting John Philip Sousa or something similar. The colors, the twirling batons, the prancing horses, the big-lipped smiling clowns, the super-shiny fire engines, the brand new ambulance and the mayor himself were all there. The excitement will be with me as long as I live!

I walk tall now, with a limp, but without crutches or braces or any other help. I am a senior citizen on the outside, but on the inside I will always be a young boy when I think of the day the bands played on, *and on, and on!*

God's Rescue Squad

1940

*T*hree months of convalescence in a body cast was the unpleasant, but necessary, aftermath of spinal surgery. My mother had asked if she could care for me at home during those months. So, the summer of 1940 was spent lying on a bed in the dining room or on a stretcher out on the porch. I have both happy and terrible memories of that time. The day God took over our local Rescue Squad and made it His own involved both kinds of memories.

I was gaining weight because of the marvelous care my mother was giving me. She was a wonderful nurse and was at her very best when she was caring for someone who was ill or incapacitated as I was. Daily she bathed me. Faithfully she carried my meals to me on a tray. Regularly she brought mid-morning and afternoon light snacks. At bedtime she had ice cream and cookies or some other special treat.

All that good food coupled with my total inactivity produced the inevitable: *I began to gain weight*. Not a lot, but enough to make my cast begin to feel a little tight. Then it became *really* tight, especially on my leg (the cast went down my right leg almost to my knee, to prevent me from ever sitting upright).

The doctors asked my parents to bring me back to Philadelphia so they could cut my cast open both on my leg and on my torso. I dreaded the ride down to Philadelphia and back, because I remembered how scrunched up I had been in the backseat of a car on my way home. It had been decidedly uncomfortable.

One day our doorbell rang. Two strangers stood there. They were very pleasant, as they explained to us that they were volunteer members of our local Rescue Squad. A brand new ambulance had recently been delivered to them and they were eager to give it a trial run. Someone had told them that I had to be returned to the hospital in Philadelphia and then brought back the same day. It would please them to take me there, if I would like.

What fun! I was carried out on a beautiful folding stretcher and lifted up into the ambulance. I could see everything! When I had been brought home, I had seen only the tops of the passing trees; now I could see through those big windows of the ambulance with ease.

How beautiful the New Jersey countryside was! Everything was a lush green. My world was wondrously expanded.

The day was a most exciting day for me, until I arrived at the hospital. They carried and wheeled me in to the admitting area and then the intern proceeded to cut my cast with huge plierlike cutters. When he cut the cast that covered my abdomen and chest, everything went fine. But when he started to cut the leg portion of my cast, the pain was horrible! I just gritted my teeth and said nothing. I resisted crying out and bore it stoically, as I thought a good boy should.

When the cast popped open, the blood was flowing, and the orthopedic assistant was horrified! "Why didn't you tell me I was cutting you?" he demanded.

To this day I have scars where those big cutters took a chunk of flesh out each time he advanced them to cut another inch of heavy cast.

They inserted a one-inch felt strip in the openings he had made in the torso and leg sections of the cast, and then rebound the cast with plaster-soaked gauze.

Ah! I could breathe more easily and not have to worry about gaining more weight.

On the way home those Rescue Squad fellows turned the shrill siren on and drove very fast for a short distance. What a thrill! I know I'll never forget the day God had a brand new ambulance and a special crew take an insignificant son of His all the way to Philadelphia and back. I guess I'll also remember to speak up if the medical personnel hurt me with one of their procedures. If it is supposed to hurt, OK. But if it isn't, I realize now, they need to know!

"A Large Room"

1946

My parents separated while I was a teenager. I quit school and found a clerical job at The American Cyanamid Company to support our little single-parent family. Sometimes I wondered who that "single parent" was—our mother or I?

There were no apartments available right after World War II. But the GIs were coming home, so a new law was passed requiring the relinquishing of any place they had previously rented. Suddenly the small apartment we had been renting had to be vacated to make way for a veteran. This meant splitting up and living in individually rented rooms. I searched diligently for a place where I could bring my fractured "family" back together again.

In answer to my earnest prayers, God made available to us the attic of a large home on Walnut Avenue in Cranford, New Jersey. That house had dormer windows on each of the four sides of the attic portion of it. One of those dormer areas had been made into a tiny bathroom. The other three opened into the one large room in the center of the attic. The entire space had been beautifully paneled. It was light, bright and cheery. We made one of the alcoves into a living room with a pull-out couch for sleeping. Another one we furnished as a bedroom. A third one became our kitchenette, complete with a hot plate and a Dutch oven for cooking.

I cannot fully describe to you the sense of relief I felt, as the head of our little family, the day we moved into that large attic room. Nor can I depict how great was the joy in my heart when in my devotions that night, I had a very specific confirmation from heaven that we were there in the will of God. My bookmark was in the Psalms. The verse that leaped out at me had never impressed me in previous readings, but it surely did that night: "Thou hast set my feet in a large room" (Psalm 31:8, KJV).

I have lived in some spacious, gracious homes in the course of my lifetime, but never have I had a stronger, sweeter consciousness of being exactly where God wanted me and had put me than that night, kneeling by my bed in that "large room" on Walnut Avenue.

Helper of the Fatherless

1946

*B*etween my earnings and what my mother earned at a small office where she worked, we were able to pay the rent and put food on the table for our little fatherless family of three. We didn't have a lot but we had enough for our daily needs, with nothing left over. So when a sudden need came up requiring extra funds (for dental work, I think it was), we just didn't have it. We asked the Lord to help us, but from *where*, and *how*? There is something in our nature that wants to help God figure out how to do it. We should not have bothered; He had already planned it years earlier.

As my mother was getting something out of her dresser drawer, she saw a box of fancy soaps that she had been saving for a long time; her tendency was to put nice things away and never use them. It was a trait that irritated us sometimes, for if we bought her a nice gown, for example, she wouldn't wear it, but would put it in a drawer and just bring it out to look at it frequently.

She thought to herself, *Does soap get old? Does it lose its fragrance eventually if you don't use it?* Musing over the properties of soap, she opened the box and to her surprise found, in addition to the bars of soap, some U.S. savings bonds that had recently matured! Mom had purchased them years earlier and then had "lost" them. A thorough search had been unproductive. We had moved three times since "losing" them, so she never expected to see them again. Now they were mature and ready to be cashed in for more than we needed to pay those dental bills! Before we had even prayed for God's help on those bills (in fact, *long* before!), He had answered by having us "lose" the bonds, so they could be found at just the right time. He was faithfully watching over this little "fatherless" family.

Without a doubt, He is "the helper of the fatherless," just as He claims to be (Psalm 10:14)!

1947-1949

The steps of good men are directed by the Lord.
He delights in each step they take.
(Psalm 37:23, TLB)

An Application of Faith

1947

*W*hat an answer to prayer it was when my parents were finally reunited! Now I could go on to fulfill my dream of studying the Bible at Nyack College in New York State. I made application and was accepted as a special student, with the provision that I must earn my G.E.D. certificate because I had no high school diploma. This had to be done along with my college studies.

It was a scary step of faith to apply for college when I had no savings at all. All my earnings had gone to support our little family of three while Dad was not with us. In filling out the application I came to a section on finances where I was asked: "How much money will you have when you register for classes?" It did not say whether I was to base my answer on facts or faith, so I chose the latter and wrote, "$500." That was a lot of money in those days; more than two-thirds of the cost of tuition and fees for an entire year. A semester in those days cost $350. My part-time job at the college would pay only forty cents an hour!

In the fall of 1947 I began my studies at Nyack, New York, about fifty miles from my home in Cranford, New Jersey. The day I left Cranford and headed for Nyack, I counted up savings, including gifts from church people. The total was *exactly* $500. I regretted that I had not had enough faith to put down $1,000!

A Needle in a Haystack

1948

*T*he Star Route bus from New York City to my home in Cranford, New Jersey was the last lap of the three-legged trip home from Bible college. I knew it would take about fifty minutes, and I wanted them to be used profitably for witnessing about Christ's work in my life. I prayed that God would guide me as to where I should sit. *Lord, You know who is ready to receive a witness; I do not*, I said in my heart, as I waited for the bus there at the Port Authority Terminal in the Big Apple.

I was the first one on the bus. Only one person followed me. I had sat near the back of the bus; he settled into a seat at about the middle of the bus. No one else joined us. *Well, at least I know to whom You want me to witness, dear Lord*, I thought, *but I haven't the slightest idea how to approach him. I can't just get up and go sit by the only other person on the bus!*

I continued my monologue with God: *Lord, I am going to be on this bus for nearly an hour. Please let there be some way I can share my faith with this young fellow.* Then I noticed that he was in a Merchant Marine uniform, like the one my brother Richard used to wear. Suddenly I realized God had answered my prayer. I left my seat and walked up to where he was.

"Hi," I said, "my brother was in the Merchant Marines, and he gave his life for his country when his ship was torpedoed. Do you mind if I sit with you and talk?"

"Not at all," he responded.

I sat beside him, thrilled that God had opened a door that seemed so tightly closed. We chatted about his branch of the service, and my brother and his little family, and a number of things, and then suddenly he exclaimed, "Oh! This is my stop!" He tugged hard on the cord hanging above the window to alert the driver to the fact that he wanted to get off, jumped to his feet and before I knew it, he was standing on the curb waving to me as the bus pulled away.

I felt terrible! I had found the way to get next to him, but had not shared a word about the Lord Jesus. It grieved me deeply. Then I began to think: *There must be some way I can continue my conversation with him, Lord Jesus. You arranged it in the first place; You can do it again.*

I thought back over the things we had talked about. For some reason he had mentioned that his birthday was on St. Patrick's Day. I couldn't even recall what had led to that tidbit of information, but that didn't matter. I knew he had gotten off in Kenilworth. I remembered also that one of the young ladies in my church lived over in Kenilworth.

As soon as I got home I phoned Marie Moeller. "Marie, did you happen to go to high school with a young fellow whose birthday was on St. Patrick's Day who is in the Merchant Marines now?"

She was intrigued by my question. "Charles," she said, "my birthday is on St. Patrick's Day, and I guess that's how I know that Brent's is, too. And he did recently join one of the branches of the service!"

She looked up his phone number in her directory and dictated it to me. I called that number. When a young man answered, I asked, "Do you happen to be the Merchant Marine beside whom I sat on the bus this morning?"

"Yes!" he exclaimed excitedly.

I continued, "I felt our conversation came to such an abrupt end that I wanted to try to find you in the hopes of continuing our visit."

Not only did we chat on the phone, but also he came over to the little church I was student pastoring in Greenpoint, Brooklyn, and there heard the gospel as I preached it. Though he made no personal commitment just then, I will not be totally surprised if in heaven Brent will reintroduce himself to me on one of the myriads of planets I plan to explore. He was not on that bus by blind chance, nor was he in Merchant Marine uniform by chance, nor did it just happen that Marie lived in Kenilworth and had a St. Patrick's Day birthday, too. God knows where each needle is in His gigantic haystack. Those He has chosen will be reached with the truth, even if He has to give unusual assistance to His ambassadors in relocating that needle when it seems irretrievably lost.

"Come on Down?"

1948

ach summer between school years at Nyack, I needed a job in order to return to college in the fall. Without work or financial reserves, there was just no way that I could go back. I was willing to do almost anything to earn the money for my education, but my summertime willingness was obviously not enough. The economy was poor and jobs were scarce. No one was hiring.

I went from one place of business to another, day after day, asking for a job. Each day was not only fruitless, but was also one more day of the short summer gone. I searched through the want ads diligently, but there seemed to be no jobs available that summer. In desperation I prayed as I opened the newspaper one morning, "Lord Jesus, if I am to return to Bible school this fall, I must have a job. Please help me today!"

One of the want ads seemed to leap right out at me. I looked more closely and the print was not any heavier than the others, though it had definitely caught my attention unexpectedly. Its wording, however, was not at all encouraging: "Experienced waitress wanted."

I did not qualify at all for that job, but I picked up the phone and dialed the number anyway. I began: "I see your ad for an experienced waitress in today's paper. I am not a waitress, as I think you can tell from my male voice, and I have no experience, but I desperately need that job if I am to return to college this fall."

There was a moment of startled silence on the line. Then the owner of the restaurant responded, "And I like your spunk. Come on down!"

I did, and I earned more money that summer working as an "experienced waitress" there at the Cranford Diner than during any other summer. It is true that "His paths [are] beyond tracing out" (Romans 11:33) and His ways are not our ways (see Isaiah 55:8).

The Spider and the Fly

1948

I deliberately skipped the noon meal in the college dining hall to have some time all alone with God in a very secluded spot I had discovered up on the mountain. Off to the side of the trail leading to the top of the mountain there was a natural altar. It consisted of a low rock on which I could kneel with a higher one beside it on which I could rest my arms while praying. I loved it there. The bushes were so thick around the spot that a hiker on the trail would not even see me as he passed by. It was my own private meeting place with God.

This day I was intent upon finding victory over something in my life that kept overtaking me no matter how hard I tried to be free from it. I knelt and wept as I prayed. Somehow it seemed as if God was not responding to me. It felt as if the heavens were made of brass; I was not able to get through to God with my prayers. I was thoroughly discouraged!

As I knelt there, deeply frustrated, through the blur of my salty tears I noticed a fly land on a web in the grass. The spider came to attention instantly, and then did nothing at all. He just waited, tense and still.

The fly rested for awhile and then tried to fly away, but his feet were caught in that sticky web. He beat the air furiously with his wings and only succeeded in getting one of his wings caught in the web! Still the spider did nothing.

The fly now beat the air frantically with his one free wing. Eventually that wing also became entangled in the web. Now all I could see was the convulsive wrenching of that fly's body as he vainly attempted to make those wings work. It was then that the spider rushed over to bind the fly with additional strands of webbing, preserving him alive but helpless. When he was ready for a meal, the spider could feed on him.

Spontaneously I intervened. I reached down with my little finger and flicked that fly free. Away he flew!

Suddenly God spoke to my heart! *You are just like that fly. You struggle and you strive and you strain and you try, but you cannot free yourself from the devil's web. The more you struggle, the more entangled you become! If you would only let Me, I could so easily set you free. It would take no great effort on my part. With My little finger I can set you free!*

I learned a never-to-be forgotten lesson that day. There is no bondage from which I cannot be delivered. My Lord, who bound the strong man and emerged from the grave eternally victorious over him, is not only able to free me, but also, can do it very easily. "All authority in heaven and on earth has been given to me" is His bold declaration (see Matthew 28:18)! "If the Son sets you free, you will be free indeed" (John 8:36)!

Your Father Knows What You Need

1948

During my years at Nyack I was most frugal. I answered letters only if the writer included a stamp! I did not buy treats at the popular "Hub." I relied totally upon care packages for my bedtime snacks. Increasingly, however, I felt a desire to take voice lessons in order to improve my ministry in my home church, and in my travels with my roommate, Doug Herbert. Doug was an excellent chalk artist. I sang and played the background music for his drawings. It did not seem right, though, for me to use $25 for the luxury of voice lessons when I was trusting God for my necessities. I prayed, "Lord, if You want me to take those lessons send me $25 in one lump sum, so that I will know that You intend it to be used that way."

The day after Christmas David Crane, one of my Sunday school boys, came to the door of our attic apartment and handed me a Christmas card. In it was a note that said, "We cut down the big Colorado spruce tree in front of our house, and I made it into wreaths and sold them. I want you to have the money. You may use it any way you want." I praised God for His faithfulness and rejoiced over this specific answer to prayer—a gift of exactly $25!

When my roommate came to pick me up to return to Bible college, he realized suddenly that he had forgotten something, so he went back to his home to get it. I went in with him and visited with his well-to-do, widowed mother. I told her what God had done and she was quite touched emotionally by the story. She reached for her pocketbook and took out a $10 bill. She said, "I want you to have this for those lessons, too."

"No, Mrs. Herbert," I insisted, "voice lessons are only $25."

"But you may need something to rent a practice room," she said.

"That's thoughtful of you, Mrs. Herbert, but they don't charge for the use of practice rooms," I countered. Suddenly the thought struck me, *What am I doing? Here is a wealthy lady trying to give me $10 and I am arguing with her.*

So when she said, "I *really* want you to have this," I responded, "Well, thank you. Thank you *very* much!"

When I enrolled for the lessons, the registrar asked me which teacher I preferred. I wanted Miss Geraldine Southern. She was the best of them all.

"Are you aware," he asked me, "that Miss Southern's lessons cost $10 more than the others?"

"No, sir," I said, "but I would still like to have Miss Southern, thank you!"

How amazing! God had known from the beginning that my need was for $35 and not $25.

"[Y]our Father knows what you need before you ask him" (Matthew 6:8).

A Jew Gives to Christian Missions

1949

My roommate had gone home for the weekend, but I stayed on at the Bible college to work on a paper. On Sunday evening during my devotions, there came a great earnestness in my spirit. I very deeply wanted to be used of God in a special way when I entered the ministry. "Lord," I prayed, "I want nothing to hinder You from using me in a really significant way. If there is anything that would block the flow of Your Holy Spirit through my life, please show that to me."

Instantly I had a flashback about something that had happened when I was a boy in high school. I had worked after school each day and all day Saturday for a man by the name of Mr. Shereshevsky. He had a confectionery store in which he sold candy and newspapers. Along one wall was a little lunch counter with three stools. I worked behind that counter making sandwiches, ice cream desserts and other things. He told me that each evening at supper time I could have fifteen cents worth of things from his store. In the 1940s that would buy a soft drink from the fountain and a cookie or candy bar. To me that seemed very stingy of him.

Sometimes people would come in to buy a newspaper. They would leave their coin on the counter and take the paper while I was busy dipping a dish of ice cream for another customer. There were a few times when I pocketed that money, and then used it to buy a little more for my supper than he had said I could. I reasoned I was not stealing; he owed me that! Anyway, the money actually went into his cash drawer. I kept none of it.

Now, suddenly, there on my knees in the Bible college, I knew those thoughts were rationalizations and I had been terribly wrong. I had stolen from him!

"Lord, I will put a $5 bill in an envelope, address it to Mr. Shereshevsky, and put no return address on it. That's two or three times as much as I stole from him. He will be getting his money back with great interest. He won't even know where it came from, but my conscience will be clear."

To my surprise, that prayer brought no peace whatsoever. When my roommate returned from his weekend at home, I told him about the way the Lord had been dealing with me. I told him I guessed I would have no peace until I had gone to see Mr. Shereshevsky to pay him back and to ask his forgiveness, though I dreaded doing that.

The more I told him, the sadder he looked. It was not that he was all that sympathetic. It was that he was remembering something *he* needed to make right, too. We decided together that we had to right those wrongs promptly. Neither of us ever took our allowed discretionary "cuts" from classes, so we had plenty of them. We decided to cut all classes the next day and make the trip together to Mr. Shereshevsky and to the person my roommate had sinned against.

We left the college early the next morning. He drove so slowly. I understood that. We were headed in the direction of the house he needed to go to first. When we arrived in front of it, he just sat there in the car.

"Go ahead, buddy; it will never get any easier!" I prodded him.

He shot me an irritated sideways glance and got out of the car. Slowly he walked up the sidewalk, and then he could not seem to find the doorbell. *I could see it from all the way out there in the car!* When he put his finger on it, he lingered long before pressing it.

The door opened; he went inside, and it closed upon him like the door of a morgue!

I sat there praying for a long time.

Eventually the door opened and out bounced my roommate. He forgot all his manners, letting the screen door slam behind him as he hurried down the sidewalk. He appeared to float about two inches above the pavement all the way to the car! He got in, slammed the car door and said, "I feel so good!"

"Oh, be quiet!" I retorted. His joy bothered me.

Now he drove on toward Mr. Shereshevsky's.

Why did he have to go so fast now? I was in no hurry to get there. When we arrived, he parked right alongside the store, and I lingered.

"Go ahead, buddy. It will never be any easier!" he mimicked me.

It was my turn to give him that sideways, irritated look.

I got out of the car and went in looking for a dark corner where I might hide while mustering up my courage.

Mr. Shereshevsky spotted me and called to his wife, "Honey, take care of this customer for me. I see Charles has come back, and I am so eager to see him!"

I thought to myself, *I wish I could say the same!*

After exchanges of greetings, I bluntly said, "Mr. Shereshevsky, I came here today especially to pay you something I owe you and to ask for your forgiveness. When I worked for you . . . "

I told him the story. It was difficult, but I had to do it. "Mr. Shereshevsky, I want to be the best pastor I can possibly be, and I cannot minister effectively with this kind of thing on my conscience."

Tears came into the old Jew's eyes. He put his arm over my shoulder and said tenderly, "I have two sons. I understand. I don't want your money."

"No, Mr. Shereshevsky, I cannot keep this," I said, "It is your money, and I really want you to take it."

"Son," he said, as he accepted my $5 bill, "as you said, this is *my* money. I can do anything with it I want to, right?"

"Yes," I acknowledged.

"OK then," Mr Shereshevsky said, "what I want to do with it is to give it to missions. You go to the Missionary Training Institute. Surely you could put this in the offering there for me."

I cried as I accepted his $5 for Christian missions! What hath God wrought? *A Jewish man giving to Christian missions!*

When I walked out to the car, I noticed that the sky was more deeply blue. It seemed to me as if the birds had never sung so sweetly. It was one of the most wonderful days of my life. I had obeyed God, and He had honored that.

Both Steps and Stops Are Ordered by the Lord

1949

I was bone weary! However, weariness was not the only feeling in my bones. There were deeply satisfying emotions as well. There was a sense of accomplishment. There was a thrill of excitement, as I anticipated the startled look on my parents' faces when they would discover what I had done for them. There was the electrifying sense of being fully alive that comes from doing something *different*. How could I know that these feelings would be overshadowed within the next hour as effectively as if we were to put Mount McKinley alongside the 4,000-foot Holston Mountain in Tennessee?

In a hectic yesterday I had completed the complicated registration process at Nyack College with uncharacteristic speed. With registration out of the way, I knew it was possible for me to accomplish the project for my parents in a single day, if I rose with the roosters. I negotiated the fifty-mile bus-subway-bus trip to my home in Cranford, New Jersey, with such beautiful synchronization that it seemed almost as if the three vehicles were running just for my convenience. *This was my day!* No question about it.

My parents were away enjoying a few days of vacation. I worked feverishly at my skills, so often applied to the homes of others, but this time used to surprise my own parents. If the wallpaper would cooperate and stay where I put it without stretching, if the match would be somewhat uncomplicated, if the quality brushes I had purchased would serve as well as I hoped they would for the painting of the woodwork, I could possibly complete their entire bedroom before the day was over.

Everything went smoothly!

When the last strip of wallpaper was hung in place, and the last brushful of white enamel paint gleamed on the baseboard, and the tools were cleaned and stored, there was hardly time for one more admiring look before dashing to the "Star Route" bus that linked my hometown with the Port Authority terminal in New York City. There was a definite similarity between the "*clunk*" of my fifty-cent piece in the change box on the bus and the "*plunk*" of my 125 pounds as I fell into my seat. I leaned my head back against the headrest and drew in three times the usual breath, holding it momentarily. Why does that feel so good when you think you are more tired than you have ever been in all your life?

It was 10:03. I raised my watch arm, rather than moving my head, and studied its face. Simple math stumbled in my brain. After a day like this one, my calculations were far from calculatorlike in speed. As a matter of fact, they were even a far cry from the old whirring, jerking, lurching Friden calculators I used to operate. But if the driver would concentrate on the road, the traffic lights between Cranford and New York City would cooperate, not too many customers would force a stop and the "A" train subway express would come at just the right moment, I *might* make that 11 p.m. bus from upper Manhattan to Nyack.

And if not? Well, the next bus would leave at midnight, one long hour later.

"Midnight!" That sounded more ominous than usual. I must have checked my watch fifty-two times in half as many minutes while the bus sped toward New York City. Yes, it *was* my day!

Everything was falling into place beautifully—the lights, the traffic, the people, the driver and even the hands on my watch. When the bus lurched to a stop in the Port Authority terminal, I was the first one out through those squeaky foldaway doors. I dashed down the subway steps with reckless abandon. I could hear the clickety-clatter of the arriving train in the tunnel below. I may even have negotiated three steps at a time in my hurry. At any rate, I was able to squeeze through those closing doors of the subway train, and to flop on one of the seats, panting, but delighted with my continuing good fortune.

The next few minutes were tense ones. The subway would have to travel right along, or I would still miss that bus. I knew those stops well—59th Street, 72nd Street, 125th Street. The 59th Street stop arrived in less time than I had allotted. "Three cheers!" I said to myself. The next stop was ahead of schedule as well. "Thank You, Lord," I prayed in my heart, aware that God had been especially good to me in every way that day.

Hold everything! Something seemed ominously wrong about this stop. I felt it almost instinctively. As the doors were closing I caught a glimpse of the station identification imbedded in the tiled walls. They were definitely not a seven and a two! The impact of my error struck me forcibly. This was not the "A" express hurtling toward the George Washington Bridge. It was the "D" express following the same tracks as the "A" train as far as 59th Street, and then veering off into the Bronx!

Painfully aware of the consequences of such an error, I got off at the next station and took a southbound "D" train back to 59th Street. There I crossed to the northbound platform to get the next "A" express that would come along. Dejected, I looked at my watch again. This wasn't my day after all, not all the way through, anyway. There was no possibility of making that bus to Nyack now, unless it was late.

The doors were hardly open widely enough at 175th Street when I forced my body through them and dashed up the stairs into the terminal just in time to watch the taillights of my bus to Nyack going down the street in the direction of the George Washington Bridge. If I had been thirty seconds earlier, I would have been praising the Lord for delaying that bus long enough for me to catch it.

What was I to think now? It seems Romans 8:28 gets overworked at times. When you are as tired as I was, it isn't all that easy to glibly spout, "Praise the Lord anyhow!" Oh well, it certainly wasn't the end of the world. In another fifty-five minutes the midnight bus would be leaving for Nyack. It would be childish to get too upset. But I was tired in every muscle and it was a bit difficult to act mature!

At 11:30 I walked out to the slot from which the Nyack bus would be leaving. *If I'm this early, I may as well get in line and enjoy a good seat*, I reasoned. While standing there, I noticed a motherly, older woman who appeared to be Scandinavian who came and stood right behind me. There was something so wholesome and gracious about her that I wondered if she knew the Lord Jesus, too.

I asked her a question I very seldom ask anyone, for the term is often misunderstood: "Are you a Christian?"

"Why, yes!" she exclaimed, "I *am* a Christian."

After some joyous visiting together, I noticed a thoughtful squinting of her blue eyes as she asked, "Where are you going?"

"To Nyack," I said.

"And when you arrive in Nyack, where are you going?"

I *loved* her Swedish accent! "Up the hill to the college," I responded.

"Oh, *praise the Lord!*" Ebba Smedborg exclaimed sincerely with delight written all over her Swedish (and sweetish) face. "I too am going up the hill. I am on my way to visit my brother, Dr. Lee Olson, who teaches at the college. I knew I had to walk through a section of town that frightens me, so I asked the Lord Jesus to send someone to walk with me."

Suddenly Romans 8:28 no longer seemed overworked or the least bit inappropriate. The glory of the living God and His interest in our lives was so very evident. God does indeed have a perfect plan for us. It even includes getting on the wrong train so you will miss the 11 o'clock bus when there is a prayer to be answered on the 12 o'clock bus! That took the weariness out of my bones.

When I arrived in my dormitory room at nearly 1 a.m. I felt the exhilaration of a day never-to-be-forgotten, rather than the bone weariness of a few hours earlier. God's will, beautifully revealed and sweetly accomplished, had added a rare perfume to that day's memory that would overshadow forever the odors of wet wallpaper and fresh enamel paint! God had so obviously intervened in my life to prove His personal interest, not just in *me*, but also in a dear child of His who had cried out to Him when she was afraid.

Faith Steps Out

1949

*T*he treasurer of Nyack Missionary College spoke to the student body very frankly. The college was in deep financial trouble, he told us. There were creditors who had to be paid without delay. "From now on, when your monthly bill for room and board is due it must be paid on the due date or you will have to go home. We can no longer carry you on our books. Hopefully, your church or friends or family will send you back to us. We are forced to do this; we hope you understand."

We did, of course, though it struck fear in our hearts. Forty dollars a month was a sizable amount in 1949. Earning only twenty-five cents an hour, the dollars did not add up quickly.

One month I counted the bills in my wallet when payment day arrived. There were only $12. I was $28 short. The morning mail brought me nothing. I knew God would have to provide in some other way. All day long I prayed and waited. Nothing happened.

I recalled that somewhere I had read the statement, "Faith steps out into the chasm, believing the rock will be there!" So, shortly before the business office closed, I knelt in my room and prayed, *Lord Jesus, I do not believe You brought me to Bible college only to have me go back home again. I am going to go down to the* *bookkeeper's office and get in that line by faith, as if I had the $40 in my wallet. I will trust You to provide the $28 I need by the time I get up to the desk.*

There were eight people in line ahead of me. *Oh, how I prayed* as I awaited my turn! I gave God all kinds of great ideas as to how He could provide the funds, but He didn't seem to be listening. I suggested that there could be a piece of my mail that had been put in another student's mailbox by mistake. That student could pick up his mail, and finding it, bring it to me. No such thing happened, however. I was directly in front of the bookkeeper's desk now. There were a half dozen in line behind me. I still had only $12. I was embarrassed.

To stall for time, I asked, "How much do I owe?" I knew full well how much I owed. I had paid nothing on that $40 responsibility as yet. She went over to the closet shelf and got out the huge ledger. Each student had a page in that ledger. She turned over those wide pages until she came to mine, ran her finger down to the bottom figure, looked up and said, "You owe $12. Someone has anonymously paid $28."

Oh, how my heart rejoiced! Only God and I knew what I had in my wallet. That was enough.

"Pennies" from Heaven

1949

I sat with my head bowed during the organ prelude one Sunday morning in my home church. I was preparing my heart for the worship service, but my prayer kept slipping back to my pressing need. *Lord Jesus, You called me to go to Bible college and prepare for the ministry. I have gotten this far along by faith. You have met my financial needs so graciously. I am so short of funds for returning from this Christmas vacation. The new semester starts soon and I am far from having the money I need to register. I pray that You will provide everything I have need of. I have done all I possibly can in the way of part-time work. I must leave the rest to You.*

The prayer was not uninterrupted, however. Partway through, an envelope softly dropped into my lap. I opened my eyes and saw the envelope but could not tell who had dropped it there. I was in the last pew. Lots of people were coming into church and were brushing past that pew.

I continued in prayer without opening it. Then I heard the flutter of another envelope falling into my lap. Once again, I could not tell who had dropped it there. Before I finished my prayer, a third one landed on top of the other two! I felt sure there would be notes inside and

I would be able to thank those wonderful church people who had helped me.

I was in for two surprises: 1) all three envelopes had cash in them, and no identification of the donor; and 2) the total of the three gifts came to exactly what I needed to be able to register for the next semester.

Now, I have heard of "pennies from heaven," but *these were not pennies!* They were substantial gifts that God had caused to float down out of dedicated hands and hearts into my lap. They might as well have come from heaven. They beautifully confirmed both my heavenly Father's call and His love.

Postscript: I graduated debt-free from Nyack after three years of trusting God month by month for the funds necessary to meet those payments. I even had enough left over to buy a good quality dark suit for use in the pulpit of that first church assignment in Greenpoint, Brooklyn, New York.

1951-1954

*The one who calls you is
faithful and he will do it.*
(1 Thessalonians 5:24)

1951

No one can fully understand how excited I was about taking that first church in Greenpoint, Brooklyn, New York. I had dreamed of pastoring since *before* I was saved. At last it was a reality! That little, run-down church in one of the worst sections of Brooklyn was a great challenge, and I plunged into it with all my heart.

I was sold on the value of the camping experience in the life of a young person, so I wanted to get as many children as possible to go either to Delta Lake, New York, or to Camp Susque in Pennsylvania. Very few of the parents could afford to send their children to camp. All I asked was permission to take them, and I determined to trust God for the funds I needed.

Eighteen children were lined up to go! That was phenomenal for our little church. So was the amount of supplemental money needed to get them there and to pay for their stay at the camps! I needed nearly $400. That was no small sum in the 1950s. I asked God to provide every cent of it.

I let the people know about my project, but for some reason the funds did not flow in. As it came closer and closer to the time to take those kids to camp, I realized increasingly that God was going to have to work a miracle, for I still lacked $300. I never dreamed He would work *two* miracles!

One Sunday I preached on the subject of tithing. I included in my sermon the text, "Will a man rob God? Yet you rob me. But you ask, 'How do we rob you?' In tithes and offerings" (Malachi 3:8). I made it very clear that God, after urging us to bring the whole tithe into His storehouse had promised: "Test me in this . . . and see if I will not throw open the floodgates of heaven and pour out so much blessing that you will not have room enough for it" (3:10).

God blessed that message. That very evening Jesse Stewart handed me an envelope as she left the church. "I have always given to the work of the Lord, Pastor," she said, "but I have kept no record of my giving, so I don't really know if I have given ten percent or not. I don't want to be guilty of robbing God. Here is an extra gift, just to be certain that I have not robbed Him. You may use it to help get those children to camp, if you would like."

In that envelope was a check for $300. God had provided all I needed to take all eighteen children to camp. My heart was full of praise!

But that was only the first miracle. The next morning Jesse went in to work at the Rockefeller Center in New York City. The big boss asked her to come into his office. That frightened her. What on earth could he want to see her for?

"Jesse," he began, "I have watched your work and I am pleased with it. I feel you have managerial capabilities. Do you think you could handle it if I made you the head of your entire department?"

Jesse was so overwhelmed that she could hardly answer. In those days it was not popular to give women such heavy responsibility. To place a woman over both men and women like this was, in fact, unheard of in the major oil company where she worked.

Jesse tried to compose herself for her answer, and then very deliberately said, "Yes, sir, I feel I could handle that."

He went on to tell her that there would be a substantial raise. In fact, in the first few months she more than made up for all she had given to God in that envelope. "[S]ee if I will not throw open the floodgates of heaven and pour out so much blessing that you will not have room enough for it" (3:10) had been God's explicit promise, and He kept it!

All Your Needs

1952

If we could only remodel that useless, un-needed balcony and make an assembly room out of it, I mused, *we would gain some badly needed space and be able to expand our program among the youth of our inner-city community.*

Our big problem was lack of funds. This was my first church after Bible school. It was an inner-city church with only a handful of people, but it was growing. No one in it was wealthy.

One of the most promising aspects of our ministry there was the responsiveness of the children in the area. We had gained the confidence of the parents and they were allowing their children to come to the things we planned for them. Our Released Time program was booming. We were the only church in Greenpoint, Brooklyn that was willing to provide such a class on Wednesday afternoons, so we got children from many different church backgrounds. Some of those young people had never heard the gospel before and they were responding beautifully. One eventually served as a missionary with The Christian and Missionary Alliance.

We had many children who came to our DVBS in the summer. Our club program was exciting. I had taken eighteen children to summer camps. That had necessitated praying in the funds for the ones who could not afford it because there was no budget for this.

Since God had so marvelously provided *those* funds, why couldn't He also send in the $3,500 needed to renovate that balcony? It was a huge sum of money in those days and our congregation was very small.

"But God is not small!" I reminded myself.

I encouraged the people to pray that He would send us the entire $3,500 by a certain date so we could give the contractor the "go ahead" signal. We took a special offering. Individuals gave gifts. Parishioners who had moved away but had heard of our plans sent checks. When it was all tallied, it came to $3,250. Our little church was filled with rejoicing!

But I was not satisfied. God had not said he would supply almost all our need; He had said "all your need!" Raising $3,250 was not a clear victory. To me it seemed like a defeat. I went to prayer alone in my little study.

The telephone rang and I was startled by who was calling, as well as by the nature of his request. He was the vice president of the biggest bank in our community, the Greenpoint Savings Bank.

"Are you able to see me for a few minutes sometime this morning, pastor?" he asked.

"Certainly," I responded, "I would be happy to come to see you."

"No," he said, "I would like to come to *your* office."

The vice president of that prestigious bank wanted to come to *my* office! *Why?* What could he possibly want?

In a few minutes the doorbell rang. As I let him in, I felt awestruck. I was a very young pastor—only twenty-one years old—and unfortunately looked so much younger than I really was. That bothered me a lot. He was an older man—back then I saw him as an "old" man, in fact! He looked very distinguished, the perfect image of a prosperous banker.

I invited him to sit down.

He wasted no time in stating his purpose. "Pastor," he said, "tell me what you offer the youth of our community."

I was happy to tell him how God was blessing our efforts to provide something meaningful for the poor, deprived children of our area. In glowing terms I told Him of the way God had prospered this outreach. I didn't miss my opportunity to squeeze in a word of witness to him personally, either.

He smiled a knowing smile and said, "I have heard all of this before, Pastor. I just wanted to hear it from you as well. Our bank is very community-minded. We care about the people we serve. Apparently you do as well. We would like to have a part in helping you with your outreach. We hear you are remodeling your balcony, and it is my pleasure on behalf of the Board of Directors of the Greenpoint Savings Bank to present this check to help you. We hope it will encourage you in the good work you are doing."

He extended his hand toward me with a check in it *in the amount of $250!* I couldn't keep the tears back. I don't think he could either, when he saw how moved I was. I told him about our lacking that precise amount! He could not miss seeing how real God is, and he must have been humbled by being the tool God had used.

When God says He will provide *all* our need according to His riches in glory by Christ Jesus, *He means all!* God doesn't use words thoughtlessly or make promises He does not intend to keep.

A Lover Laughs at Locksmiths

1952

My buddy, Paul Mills, was being married in Boston. He had given me the honor of being his best man. However, in 1950, the bus connection between Boston and Brooklyn, where I was pastoring, was not good. There were no freeways, fast trains nor shuttles yet, so getting there required spending eight long hours on the road.

As I boarded the Greyhound bus in New York City, I prayed, *Lord Jesus, I am going to be riding this bus all day long. Please help me to choose a seat where my seatmate will be open to my witness.* I chose to sit beside a young man who looked to be either in high school or perhaps a freshman in college. I was twenty-two and had my college experience behind me; that might afford us some common interest on which to base a conversation.

"Hi," I said, as I struggled to squeeze my bag into the overhead luggage rack.

"Hello," he barely responded, and turned to look out the window.

As I settled into my seat, I continued, "Where are you headed?"

"Boston," was his one-word answer, turning away from me again.

"Great! I'm headed there too!" I said enthusiastically.

"Oh," he grunted, and turned to look out the window.

Almost anything I said to him elicited a one-word response and a body language that almost shouted, "I don't want to talk, so stop bothering me." I realized that pressing the issue would be counterproductive, so I didn't say anything further. Instead I began to pray for him. *Lord Jesus, I am going to be sitting next to this fellow for the next eight hours and I want to witness to him. I can't witness to someone who will not even talk to me. Please open this door somehow. I don't see how, but nothing is impossible with You!*

At one point, the young fellow reached under the seat for his satchel and rummaged in it for something. In the process, he pulled out his camera and then replaced it. Etched on the camera case was a name and address: "Byron Blanchard, 1234 Douglas Street, Omaha, Nebraska." (I don't remember the actual street numbers, but it *was* Douglas Street.)

An hour or more passed monotonously. The drone of the motor made the boy sleepy and he dozed off for thirty minutes or more. While he was asleep the weather changed from brilliant sunshine to overcast to soft drizzle.

He stirred, then looked in my direction as he reoriented himself to his surroundings.

I said, "Did you have a good sleep?"

"Yep," he said and turned to look out the window, again rejecting my attempt at conversation.

"The weather changed while you were sleeping, By-ron." (I deliberately used his name)

His head spun back toward me. He looked at me intently as he responded, "Yes, I noticed."

"Well, we can't have sunshine all the time, can we, Byron?"

Again, the use of his name triggered an almost involuntary pivoting of his head toward me.

"I'm headed to Boston for the wedding of my friend. What draws you to Boston?" I queried.

"Well, I'm making a trip around the country to visit various colleges to try to decide where I want to study when I finish high school this year."

"That's terrific, Byron!" I said, noticing how closely he looked at my facial features each time I used his name. "What do you look for on the various campuses?"

He responded with a clear set of criteria he considered important. "I ask for a handbook, of course, and study the prerequisites for acceptance into the college or university. I also look over the facilities and research the reputation of the faculty. I ask the students how they feel about their college."

"Byron, you mentioned *prerequisites*. What do you think the prerequisites for getting into heaven are?"

He was thoughtful for a moment, and then responded, "I guess I never considered that!"

"Where you go to college is a very significant decision," I continued. "So is where you go after you finish your life here on earth. Are you familiar with the fact that God has published a handbook that spells out the prerequisites for entry into Heaven, and that His rules are very explicit?"

"I never thought about it that way," he admitted.

"What would your guess be as to what God's entrance requirements are?" I asked.

He paused for a moment and then thoughtfully responded, "I suppose it is important to live a good moral life, to join a church and to treat your neighbor well."

"Those are good things to do, Byron, but they aren't enough, according to the handbook. I have that handbook with me in my briefcase," I said, noticing that the use of his name had triggered again a careful study of my face. "Mind if I point out some of those prerequisites?" I asked.

"No, not at all," he said, rather obviously intrigued by this analogy. I had the joy of explaining the way of salvation as clearly as I knew how, turning from passage to passage to reveal how God had lovingly spelled out what His prerequisites are. I wish I could say I led him to Christ before he got off the bus that day. I cannot.

He was a very thoughtful and methodical person who did his homework and thought things through. He was not about to make a decision on the spur of the moment. I still hope to have him come up to me in heaven someday and say, "Do you by any chance remember a Byron Blanchard from Omaha who sat by . . ." I will have him in my arms in a big bear hug before he ever finishes that sentence and will cherish the moment as one of the greatest serendipitous experiences of heaven.

Oh, by the way, when we got off the bus in Boston and went our separate ways, Byron shook my hand warmly, thanked me for our conversation and said, "Uh, before we part, one final question: How did you know my name?"

I told him about his camera case, but my answer wasn't the whole truth. I didn't tell him about my cry for help to a God with whom nothing is impossible, who can open any closed door, no matter how sturdy the locks. Shakespeare wrote, "A lover laughs at locksmiths." In this instance, the greatest love-giver of all picked the lock adroitly.

Cast Your Bread upon the Waters

1952

I worked really hard in my first pastoral assignment. I was a bachelor and totally committed to serving both my Lord and Faith Gospel Church there in Greenpoint, New York. I thought nothing of putting in sixteen to eighteen hours a day. I loved it!

My dedication to the work took its toll physically without my realizing at first what was happening. When I completely forgot a speaking engagement for which I had faithfully prepared, but then failed to show up at the college at the appointed time, I was terribly embarrassed. I had reviewed the night before and felt honored to be invited there by that Campus Crusade group, but somehow I forgot.

The following week the same thing happened at another college with an InterVarsity group. I was not only embarrassed this time, *I was scared!* I knew something was going wrong with me and concluded that it was important for me to go away for a complete rest. I made arrangements to take a train to Florida where I could stretch out on the sand and drink in the sunshine day after day for a couple of weeks. A complete rest would hopefully refresh me and reverse this frightening trend toward early Alzheimers!

When it came time to leave, George Meisenheimer, the treasurer of our church, said, "Pastor, I have decided to pay you for three weeks instead of two. This is for the two weeks you are gone and the first week after you get back."

"Well that's nice of you, Mr. Meisenheimer," I said. I divided the money, putting away some for rent and other things, but because I was a bachelor pastor those first five years, my food money went into my pocket.

I left for the Southland. My food money held out wonderfully. I had three good meals each day plus two Dairy Queen "blizzards" (thick, *very* thick milkshakes), and still I had money left over when I returned to my pastorate in Brooklyn. Suddenly I realized why my money had held out so well. I had been spending three weeks' food money in two weeks' time. There was no paycheck coming. I had already been paid.

I sat down at the table in my small apartment and counted my remaining money, dividing the sum by seven. I quickly concluded it was not enough to hold body and soul together for a week. Then I remembered a *Reader's Digest* article that had authoritatively stated that peanut butter is as nourishing as meat. It has lots of protein, the article had pointed out. I decided I should buy a big jar of peanut butter and a long loaf of thin-sliced sandwich bread. For the next twenty-one meals, I could live off peanut butter sandwiches.

Then the whole thing struck me funny and I started to laugh. Here I was, a child of the King, and I was planning to live on peanut butter sandwiches for a week. *Who ever heard of a prince that had to exist on peanut butter sandwiches?* I enjoy peanut butter, but the thought of that much for that long brought only one word to my mind—Yuk!

I went to my knees. *Dear Lord*, I said, *I did not do this deliberately. I have made a serious but honest mistake. Would You be so gracious as to send me another $6 to add to what I now have?*

I realize that $6 is not very much these days, but in 1952 it certainly was adequate when added to what I already had. I was not asking extravagantly, but I was praying for enough.

Less than two hours later my telephone rang. The caller was a godly lady from our congregation. Mrs. Delena was the wife of a New York City fireman. After chatting awhile, Kay said to me, "Pastor, I am somewhat embarrassed to ask you this question, but while I was having my devotions this morning I felt as though God said clearly to me, 'Give Pastor Shepson $6.' Do you have some need for six dollars?"

I was almost speechless! "Why, Kay, not two hours ago I specifically asked God for $6." I told her the story. We both were thrilled. I was, because He had so wonderfully heard my prayer. She was, because God had trusted her by speaking directly to her mind and heart.

"I'll send it right over with Gracie, Pastor."

She did, and I had all I needed for that week.

But that is not the end of the story, nor the most thrilling part of it, in fact! Twelve years later when I was preaching in my home church at Cranford, New Jersey, I used the incident as an illustration of how God takes care of His children, and how real He wants to be to us.

After the service a rather strange man came up to me. (God has all kinds of faithful children, even some strange ones.) As he shook my hand, he blurted out gruffly and rather loudly, "Did you ever pay that lady back?"

I was startled by his question and the loud, abrupt manner in which he spoke. "Why, uh, no, I didn't. I don't think she intended that I should." I was becoming a bit defensive, I realized, but the words were already out.

"I want you to!" he insisted, firmly.

Only then did I realize that he was pressing something into my hand as he was shaking it. I looked. It was $6! Now, I'm not certain where that puts me with *him*!

That afternoon I wrote Kay Delena a letter: "I don't really understand this, Kay. I feel quite certain that you *gave* me the money and did not intend that I should repay it, but this is what happened this morning [I rehearsed the experience.] So I am enclosing the $6 the man gave to me."

A few days later a tear-stained letter came in response: "Oh, dear pastor, God is *so* good! *I* had a need for $6! I had a doctor's bill to pay and lacked that amount. I prayed and said, *Lord, it is not honoring to You for me to owe this doctor's bill. Would You send me $6 so I can pay it in full?* Your letter with the $6 came in the mail that very day!"

The personal interest God takes in the plight of His children is phenomenal. When He said, "Cast your bread upon the waters, for after many days you will find it again" (Ecclesiastes 11:1), God meant it!

Delicious Dessert

1952

As a young bachelor pastor, I was often invited for dinner, especially to the homes of those who had eligible daughters. On a Sunday afternoon, I was enjoying such a meal in a home in Brooklyn, New York, when the telephone rang. The call was for me.

Mrs. Hugo, the lady on the line spoke with a Spanish accent. She sounded desperate! "Pastor Shepson, the lights will not work here at the church, and we are preparing for the Spanish service. Can you help us?"

"I'll be right there," I promised, as I was only three blocks from the church. I left the table without having dessert and hurried over to help them. The first thing I did was to check the fuse box. Everything looked all right and there were no burned fuses, so I threw the main switch to the "off" position and then immediately back on. All the big sanctuary lights lit up at once.

"Pastor, I know to do that. We tried that many times and nothing happened!" Mrs. Hugo exclaimed in embarrassment.

I lived right across the street from the church. Instead of returning to the home where I had been a guest to have my dessert, I crossed the street to my own apartment. The moment I walked in the door the telephone began ringing. It was Jimmy Jones, a young

Roman Catholic catechist who had been studying the Bible with me in private sessions.

"I am so thankful you are home, Pastor," he said. "I came to this phone booth and before dialing I prayed, *God, if You are as real as Pastor Shepson seems to think, please, please let him be home right now. I need him so badly!*"

Through unusual circumstances God had brought me back to my apartment so that I would be there in answer to Jimmy's prayer, and so he might know just how real God is. I enjoyed telling him what God had done in order to answer his prayer. Jimmy was deeply impressed. That was a sweeter dessert for me than anything my hostess might have served that day as a climax for Sunday dinner.

This Is What I Believe!

1952

Every Friday night and every Sunday night, after the evening service, we carried the portable organ and bundles of gospel tracts down to a busy intersection only two blocks from the church I pastored in Brooklyn, New York. Our faithful little group would then hold a gospel service, or "street meeting" as it was called in those days. The area was ninety-seven percent Roman Catholic and they were forbidden to come to our church. In fact, the Monsignor told the people we had a cross buried in the sill, and if they came in they would be stepping on the cross! Since they wouldn't come, we had to go out to them.

One night I handed a pamphlet to one in the crowd who had stopped momentarily to see what was going on. She was not really interested, but at least she did not throw it on the ground like some people did when they found out it was not Roman Catholic literature.

Judy Benjamin took the tract home and tossed it on her dresser. Her sister, Barbara, came home and saw the pamphlet lying there. She picked it up, read it and thought to herself, *This is what I believe!* Barbara attended a liberal church one block from the church I pastored, right on the same street. She went faithfully, but never heard the plan of salvation until she was invited to go to a Word of Life rally, conducted by Jack

Wyrtzen, over in New York City. There she had responded to the gospel message, receiving the Lord Jesus personally. She returned to her liberal church and for the next year did not grow at all. Now she was face-to-face with the gospel truth again, and she was thrilled.

On the back of the pamphlet we had stamped our church's name, address and service times. Our next meeting was to be the Wednesday evening gathering. Barbara was there! From that night on she never missed a Sunday service or a prayer meeting, or anything else, for that matter!

Her parents were not at all happy about how religious she had become, nor that she had left their church, but they tolerated it. After all, she was an adult, getting her master's degree at Queens College, and there wasn't a whole lot of authority they felt they could exercise along those lines; that is, until she announced to them that she felt called to go to the mission field and wanted to attend Nyack Missionary College for the training required by The Christian and Missionary Alliance. That was the organization under which she felt God wanted her to serve.

That angered her parents! "We paid for your education, and we expect you to use it in this country! If you want to go to South America and must go to that religious college first, then we will require you to pay us back every cent we have invested in your education before you have our permission."

They did not reckon with their daughter's determination. She got a job and reimbursed them for every cent they had put into her education and then she went off to Nyack Missionary College!

After completing her training, Barbara prepared to leave for Ecuador. Her parents made it very clear that they were not at all happy about it but did not forbid her to go. When the time came for her departure, I and a little group of believers from our church met at New York's LaGuardia Airport to see her off. We had prayer together and with our eyes filled with tears, we waved good-bye.

Barbara Benjamin tried to serve the Lord in Quito, but excruciating headaches brought on by the high altitude of that capital city simply would not let up. She had to go down to the coastal, sea-level city of Guayaquil to get relief, and eventually was assigned there to serve at the Seminario, both because of her educational qualifications and because of the inability of her body to adjust to the altitude in Quito with its elevation of nearly two miles.

For many years Barbara served in the Alliance Bible Seminary in Guayaquil most effectively, and then returned to New York City where she became the founder and president of The Spanish Bible Seminary. There, pastors are trained to serve Spanish-speaking churches in the United States and elsewhere.

Just think! It all began with the handing of a piece of gospel literature to someone who wasn't particularly interested in what it had to say. God was in that simple act of tract distribution and used it to further His own wonderful purposes for reaching Spanish-speaking people both in Ecuador and in the United States.

A Tale of Two Cities

1952

I was afraid that three consecutive weeks was too long to be away from my little church in Greenpoint, Brooklyn, New York. It was my first pastorate and I was probably overly protective of that special group of sincere believers who met there. The annual Council of The Christian and Missionary Alliance was to convene in Long Beach, California that year. The church always gave me a week to attend, wherever it was held, and they gave me a two weeks' vacation as well. I somewhat reluctantly decided to combine them and drive the 3,000 miles, going out by a southern route and coming back over a somewhat northerly one. It was before the days of freeways, and the odyssey appealed to my adventuresome spirit.

"California, here I come," I sang with gusto around my bachelor apartment. The drive across the continent was exciting, but I did miss the church people. Every Saturday night I sent a "night letter" to them by Western Union. They allowed fifty words and delivered the telegram the following morning.

From California I wrote a letter to the congregation, addressing it to the one who would be conducting the service that Sunday morning. When I signed off, I used a wording I had never in all my life used before, nor have I since. I signed it, "Your fellow pilgrim and stranger here," thinking of the text, "These . . . confessed that they were strangers and pilgrims on the earth" (Hebrews 11:13, KJV).

When I returned from California, the parishioners told me with excitement about the Sunday that letter came to the congregation. They said it was read a little late in the service and that in the earlier part of the worship time, Charles Alsdorf, a police captain from New York City, had used his beautiful bass voice to provide the special music for the service. He had chosen to sing, "I'm a Pilgrim and I'm a Stranger." Then my letter was read with the conclusion, "Your fellow pilgrim and stranger here." The congregation was awestruck. They realized that God was surely wanting them to think about that text.

Someone with a huge amount of "faith" in his atheism might label that "coincidence." I cannot. I believe God directed a Charles in Brooklyn, New York on the East Coast to sing the words and a Charles in Long Beach, California on the West Coast to sign his letter with the same words so that His own message would impact His little group of sincere, but pastorless, worshipers that morning.

Love at First Sight!

1952

I didn't believe in it! I made that clear to anyone who asked me how I felt about "love at
first sight." It made no sense. To love someone you have to know that person, *really* know him or
her.

Love is a growing thing that blooms with great
beauty, but comes to that point of beauty over a period
of time. To love someone you have never seen before
is giving dangerous permission to infatuation. Being
swept off your feet in this manner does not speak well
of your character.

Those were some of the opinionated thoughts that
readily came to my mind when the subject arose, as it
seldom did. Oh, I wasn't obnoxious about it. I kept
those thoughts to myself and only expressed them to
others when asked . . . *thankfully!*

I was a bachelor pastor. My days in Bible college
had been very busy ones with a heavy academic load
and a heavy workload, so I had not had a lot of time
for dating. I dated some lovely girls but became convinced that none of them was God's choice for me.

I didn't like bachelorhood. I wanted a wife and partner with whom to share my life and ministry. I could not
understand why God had not brought the right person
across my path. I prayed earnestly and often about it. I

fantasized about the girl of my dreams. She would be very feminine, *every inch a lady*. She would be someone I could be proud of, not so much for her facial beauty as for the beauty of her character and her walk with God. It would be wonderful if she could play the piano, too. That's not a qualification for a good pastor's wife, but it certainly would be a plus. I was not so demanding as to feel that unless a person met all of those qualifications, she would never be my wife! I said they were my idealistic fantasies, and I recognized them to be just that. I was quite prepared to modify them, for I was not so egotistical as to consider myself ideal husband material!

We planned a series of meetings in the church I pastored in Brooklyn, New York. It would add a lot to the services if special musicians from Nyack College would come down to the city to help us. I wrote a letter to Gilbert Johnson, the professor who headed up the Christian Service Department there at Nyack, asking for a duet, trio or instrumentalists. He assigned a ladies' trio along with their lady pianist. Four girls were coming to our church for that Sunday. That concerned me a bit, for even in those days traveling on the subways in New York City was not completely safe. The fact that the four would be traveling together was helpful, for there is some safety in numbers.

My final decision was to meet those girls when their bus arrived at the bus station near the George Washington Bridge, and to escort them through the maze of tunnels and train changes to get to my Greenpoint, Brooklyn church. The moment I saw the four of them, one struck my fancy so forcefully that I was overwhelmed! I guess the words "swept off my feet" would have been appropriate. That troubled me, but there was no denying the feelings in my heart.

She was one of the most beautiful women I had ever seen. Her bearing was so ladylike. The beauty of Christ shone through her countenance. Without any question, she was the girl of my dreams, right there in front of my eyes! Can you imagine my delight when I discovered that she was the pianist for the trio, and could she ever play! How thrilled I was!

Morning and night at the services I hoped the church people didn't notice how often my eyes wandered toward the piano. I simply could not help it. After the evening service, I delivered them safely to their Nyack-bound bus up by the George Washington Bridge. As I returned home on those subways, I reminisced about her beauty, her piano playing and her ladylikeness. I was absolutely enthralled. I wrestled with my strong convictions that *there is no such thing as love at first sight!*

I hurried back to my bachelor apartment and on my knees asked the Lord to forgive me for feeling so strongly about someone I had never met before. But He didn't! In fact, He wouldn't even cooperate by helping me to get rid of those "unreasonable" feelings!

I telephoned a friend of mine at Nyack whose name was so appropriate to this story—Paul Valentine! "Paul, they sent a pianist down to my church this weekend by the name of Elaine Campbell. I need to know some things about her, because I would like to ask her for a date, if everything works out all right. Is she going steady with anyone? Is she in the missions department? Could you do some checking on those two things for me? Oh, and what kind of a reputation does she have among the students?"

Paul immediately told me that she had a second-to-none testimony, and that he didn't think she was going steady with anyone, but he would check that out right away.

I should explain why I wanted to know if she was in the missions department. It was because I had a strong conviction that I should never date anyone in that department. I was called to be a pastor and not a missionary, and I felt I had no right to interfere with God's call to a girl who was preparing for the mission field.

It wasn't long before Paul called back. "All the lights are green!" he informed me enthusiastically. "She is in the Christian Education Department. She has lots of dates but refuses to go steady with anyone. Go ahead and ask her for a date."

I did.

She accepted! I was so excited I could hardly sleep. We went to the magnificent flower show in New York City and followed that by having dinner together. When I returned her to Nyack, my heart was *so* thrilled. She was everything I had ever wanted! I went back to my little apartment and wrote her a letter that night that went something like this:

My Dear Sweetheart:

I don't see how I could possibly love you more than I do already! You are the girl of my dreams, and I know God has brought you to me in answer to my earnest prayers. One year from now I plan to give you the engagement ring, after we have

had a year to learn more and more about each
other. When I do, I will give you along with it this
letter that I wrote the night of our first date!

A year later, she accepted my proposal! I gave her a
ring and the letter written the night of our first date. And
I kissed her for the very first time. I had never kissed anyone I had dated before. I had saved that kiss for the girl I
would marry. The setting was romantic. We were in the
back of a sleek speedboat that was racing across the waters of Cayuga Lake in the Fingerlakes region of New
York State. Perhaps it was symbolic of the many travels
we would enjoy together as we lived life in the fast lane
for the next forty years. We would travel in nearly that
many countries, actually!

Through those forty years Elaine was my sweetheart
and I was hers. All of our life together I continued to be
as thrilled with her as I was back then. We were very,
very happy. God brought us together through His own
wonderful planning, for which I will be eternally grateful.

I firmly believe that God, in His own time, will bring
into each life the person of His own choosing, if he or
she prays faithfully about it and listens to His voice with
a willingness to follow His leading. It probably won't be
"love at first sight." If it seems to be, that should be thoroughly checked out. I did, very thoroughly. I went to her
home to see how she responded to her parents. I
watched how she helped prepare the meal and clear the
table and help with other things. We spent lots of time
together, but not excessive time, though there was, of

course, that temptation. We prayed together. We shared dreams and expectations.

It took almost that whole year to convince Elaine that I was the one for her. It was not "love at first sight" so far as she was concerned. She was cautious, and I respected and appreciated her for it. God was so good to us both. We were exceedingly happy together, through good times and bad. Even when she lay dying in her hospital bed there in our little home in Colonial Acres, our love was stronger than ever, beautiful and sustaining.

We faithfully kept the sacred vows we made to each other at the altar in the church in Endicott, New York. We *"loved and cherished"* each other *"in sickness and in health"* until death parted us, as we had said we would. For forty-one years I loved her. Two prior to our marriage, and thirty-nine years together before she was called up into heaven ahead of me. For all those years she was the darling of my heart.

Choosing a life's partner is the second most important decision in anyone's life. Young person, don't make a mistake. Early in life make it one of your prayer requests that God will bring exactly the right person to you. There is only one! God will gladly tell you when the right time comes, if your heart is right and you have made it a habit to listen for the "gentle whisper" in your ear.

Pressed Down, Shaken Together, Running Over

1954

I don't know where it came from, but deep within me there was a strong feeling that the groom should be the one to plan a honeymoon for his bride. I wanted ours to be very special, because Elaine was so wondrously special to me! I thought it would be exciting to take her to Florida where I had enjoyed such a restful and restoring time. She had never seen palm trees and tropical flowers and the beauty of those beaches. It would be a thrill to do that together.

I saved diligently and everything was going along well until I heard an impassioned plea from a missionary who ministered in Laos. He said that the doors of that country could be closing soon and his burden was to get a gospel into every home in the country before they did. The only thing stopping him from reaching that goal was lack of funds. I had a serious talk with Elaine about whether or not I should contribute my savings for our honeymoon to that worthy cause. I suggested that if we could go somewhere right in our home state to save on travel funds, we could contribute that money for the purchase of Scriptures. She was most willing for that! I loved her even more for her level of dedication.

The honeymoon I planned was a surprise for her. When our reception was finished, we drove all the way to our cottage right on Lake George in beautiful eastern New York State. It was a simple cottage, but it had lovely views of the lake with its many islands. Our days there were wonderful. We enjoyed the fall colors, a cruise on the lake and just the joy of being together and belonging completely to each other. Our joy was full!

Now, what about that Florida honeymoon? Did we give up anything? There is a passage where Jesus told a large crowd of His disciples this: "Give, and it will be given to you. A good measure, pressed down, shaken together and running over, will be poured into your lap. For with the measure you use, it will be measured to you" (Luke 6:38).

No, we didn't really give up a thing. For a starter, we had a most enjoyable honeymoon in a resort that was not at all busy. The tourist season was nearly over. We did not have to travel far before we were settled in our comfortable cottage. We had the joy of knowing that our Florida funds were being used to share the gospel with those who might not have heard without our "sacrifice."

But there is another part to the verse. God's promise is that when we give to Him, He gives back to us "pressed down, shaken together and running over." He fulfilled that promise lavishly! We may not have gone to Florida on our honeymoon, but we eventually visited that sunny state over twenty times. In addition to visiting Florida, over the years we were able to visit over twenty different states and over twenty-five different countries together. We were able to visit many places more than once, and we didn't have to pay one cent for the facilities on most of our trips.

Can you see that God means what He says when He uses those superlatives: "Pressed down, shaken together and running over"? God never exaggerates. He keeps His promises fully. We never "sacrificed" our dream honeymoon. We only *thought* we did. It was simply *postponed* to be enjoyed over and over in later years, through the kindness of our loving Lord.

1956-1958

*. . . so shalt thou dwell in the land,
and verily thou shalt be fed.
(Psalm 37:3, KJV)*

The Winnie Cha Estate

1957

We were eager to establish a gospel-preaching church in the old/new village of Commack, Long Island. It had been mostly potato fields and farms, but suddenly houses were springing up like mushrooms, virtually over-night. Literally thousands of homes were planned by the various construction companies.

My parishioners from the church I was serving in West Hempstead, Long Island caught the vision I shared with them. Together we started afternoon services in the Commack fire hall. It was tiring, but our little group be-gan to grow. We looked everywhere for the permanent facility we needed.

Then one day as we were driving on a major side road we saw impressive, stately entrance gates to a large edi-fice that sat on a knoll. There on eight acres of land, sur-rounded by new developments, sat a lovely mansion. We had heard a rumor about an eleven-bedroom, twenty-two-room, imposing mansion that was available. Could this be it?

I went to see a local realtor about the house. He said he had heard Mrs. White was asking something like $130,000 for the mansion. In 1957 that was a *huge* sum of money. And, since we had only $27 saved, it was an astronomical figure to us!

Through various sources we learned that Mrs. Winslow White, the widowed owner of the mansion, had been offered $80,000 cash by a man of questionable reputation, who also happened to be the Bishop of Long Island for his denomination. We heard that she was both insulted by the low offer and repulsed by the idea of his carrying on his love affairs in her elegant mansion. As for his offer, she felt $130,000 was already a rock-bottom price to be asking.

Actually, she was right. The mansion was worth much more than that. She was also right about the Bishop's reputation. He was involved with one of the married women in his Bishopric, and that was offensive to many of the more sincere in his denomination.

In my devotions, I prayed earnestly about that mansion.

One morning my devotions turned out to be an amazing dialogue between my own heart and the Lord. The Scripture text of Psalm 37 and my responsive thoughts went something like this: "Fret not thyself because of evildoers, neither be thou envious against the workers of iniquity" (37:1, KJV).

But, Lord, it is difficult to accept the fact that this man who is known for his wicked ways actually has $80,000 to offer, and we have so little. It is not easy to avoid fretting!

"Trust in the LORD, and do good; so shalt *thou* dwell in the land" (37:3, KJV, emphasis added). (The word "thou" leaped right out!)

But, Lord, we have thought that an unmarried student fresh out of Nyack College would be a more logical choice, for he would not have as many financial needs. We have a little baby. If we go without a meal once in awhile, that would not matter. But the baby would not understand if we have nothing for him.

"[V]erily, thou shalt be fed" (37:3, KJV) was what I read next!

I can't believe that's the next statement in this Psalm! It's almost as if You know my thoughts and are speaking right out loud to me!

> Commit thy way unto the LORD; trust also in him; and he shall bring it to pass. . . . Rest in the LORD, and wait patiently for him: fret not thyself because of him who prospereth in his way, because of the man who bringeth wicked devices to pass. . . . For evildoers shall be cut off: but those that wait upon the LORD, they shall inherit the earth. (37:5, 7, 9, KJV)

Lord, I really want that property, and I have very little, but I am no match for him in approaching Mrs. White! That "evildoer" has $80,000 cash, and I have so little.

"A little that a righteous man hath is better than the riches of many wicked. . . . Wait on the LORD, and keep his way, and he shall exalt thee to inherit the land" (37:16, 34, KJV).

I was so excited that I bounced up the two flights of steps from my basement study to our second-floor bedroom to tell Elaine with enthusiasm and certainty, "The Winnie Cha Estate is ours! God has told me so!" I read the Scriptures to her. We were both *very* excited.

The next day we drove out to Commack. We went right to the realtor, to tell him we were definitely interested in the Winnie Cha Estate and that I would like to approach Mrs. White through him.

He laughed at me! "The Winnie Cha Estate has been sold," he said with a haughty, knowledgeable air.

I was *so* disappointed. How could this be? The Scriptures had been so clear! I went back out to the car to tell Elaine what he had said. As we sat there together in the car, I recalled a book I had read recently by Norman Grubbs—*Rees Howells, Intercessor*. In it he had told about Mr. Howells' strong conviction that God had promised the adjacent property to him. He instructed his friend to go negotiate for its purchase. His friend replied, "It has been sold." Rees Howells was so sure of the Word of God to his heart that his immediate response was, "It has *not* been sold! Go make arrangements to purchase it!"

Oh, how I wished I had that kind of faith. But I couldn't do it. *I was no Rees Howells!* Instead, I said, "Honey, let's go drive up there. It can't do any harm."

The big entranceway had a sign by it that said "Private Property. No Trespassing." I drove in through the gates anyway and circled up and around in front of the building where there was a small traffic circle.

We decided not to inquire after all, but as we were driving past the front door, it opened and a servant came out. "May I help you?" she enquired.

"Well, we were interested in the possibility of purchasing this home, but we hear it has been sold."

"No!" she exclaimed. "It has *not* been sold. Would you like to come in and meet Mrs. White?"

We were amazed! It was so similar to what had happened to Rees Howells. We parked our car near the tennis courts and carried the baby into the mansion with us in his little portable bassinet.

"Mrs. White is being bathed by her personal maid at the moment. I will take you out into the sun parlor and you can wait for her there."

She led us through a huge formal living room and down a step into the sun parlor which was just as large, but with massive windows on two sides, French doors all along another side and a mammoth fireplace along the wall it shared with the living room. We sat in big wicker furniture and waited for Virginia White. *We were terribly nervous!*

The butler brought a huge three-foot log and prepared to build a fire. The cook brought fresh fruit in elegant little dishes for us to enjoy with Mrs. White when she came down from having her bath. It was all so completely foreign to our humble lifestyle. There were five servants in all!

Mrs. White made her grand entrance. She descended the wide, circular staircase, smoking a cigarette which was plugged in to the end of the longest cigarette holder I had ever seen. Her servants were very attentive. We sat in front of the fire and told her about our desire to start a church in the community, and that we felt her lovely home would make a wonderful church and parsonage combination.

"What denomination are you with?" she asked.

God helped me with the answer, for I knew that The Christian and Missionary Alliance was not well-known on Long Island. It even had a sound too similar to

"Christian Science" to suit me. "We are with The Christian and Missionary Alliance," I said. "It is an alliance of Christians of many denominations to send out missionaries. It was started by a Presbyterian minister in New York City by the name of Dr. Albert Simpson."

I had no way of knowing that she was a Presbyterian, and this was precisely the right thing to say!

"I see that you have a *Reader's Digest* here on the coffee table that can tell you something about the work of our denomination. There is a fascinating article in it entitled, 'The White Man Comes to Shangri La.' "

I found the article for her. I could tell she was impressed. Silently I thanked the Lord for having one of the servants place that *Reader's Digest* there.

"Well, why don't I have one of the servants show you through the house?" Mrs. White said. "But before she does, I want you to know that I have been thinking about the sale of the Winnie Cha Estate. I simply want to walk out of it, leaving everything behind. That means that I am no longer willing to sell just the house. All the furnishings must be purchased along with it."

My heart sank. These new conditions for purchase were disheartening to us. There were antiques everywhere, including a Knabe baby grand piano.

The servant guided us through all the rooms. There were five main bedrooms, each with a full bath, in addition to the six bedrooms in the servants' wing. Those five main bedrooms would make a wonderful apartment for us to live in. There would still be two bathrooms for the church people to use. The other six bedrooms were just the right size for Sunday school classes.

On the way back through the living room, I asked the servant if Elaine might play the piano.

She hesitated, then asked Mrs. White if it would be all right.

Once again there was hesitation. I wondered if the soundboard was cracked, or something else was wrong with it.

Mrs. White said reluctantly, "Well, I suppose so!"

Elaine whispered, "What shall I play?"

I said, "Play, 'I Want Thy Will, O Lord.'"

I wept as she played.

So did Mrs. White! We could see the tears in her eyes when we left the piano and went on out to where she was sitting on the porch. *Why the tears?* we wondered.

We felt it was time to leave. I told her we would come back with a bona fide offer, if she would like.

She said, "No, I would like some time to think about this. I have an offer now, but it is from someone whose life is far from what it should be. I don't want him to live in my home. Let's talk some more about it next week. Come back and see me then."

Before we left I said, "May we have prayer with you, Mrs. White?"

She seemed uncomfortable with that, or was it I who was uncomfortable and insecure about having suggested it?

She agreed.

I prayed for wisdom for her and for us, then we left. *Oh, how thrilled we were!* (Elaine and I, with our $27 in the bank; "a little that a righteous person has. . . .") We knew we were not righteous on our own, but Jesus

Christ had been made righteousness unto us, the Bible said!

Our next trip to the Winnie Cha Estate was with ambivalent feelings. We were both excited and frightened. Had we done the wrong thing by asking to play that piano? Was she disturbed about my acting like her pastor and praying with her?

Our fears were groundless; before we left she said, "There are two things I want you to be sure to do before you go today: play something for me, and pray with me."

How could I dream that one day I would be praying with her the most important prayer she could ever pray? But wait! I am getting way ahead of my story. Mrs. White had a number of questions for us during this visit. She wanted to know more about how we would use the building and she was eager to know more about The Christian and Missionary Alliance. She also wanted to know how much we felt we could offer.

That was the question I was dreading. "We don't have very much money, Mrs. White," I said, gulping (if she only knew what an understatement *that* was!), "but we believe God can help us raise $40,000." That was half of what she had already been offered and the Bishop had the cash to back it up. It was also less than one-third of what she was asking.

To my amazement, she never batted an eye! "I'll need to think about that," she mused. Then she said, "You know, I really want you to have this house. I don't want that wicked man living here!"

Before we left, she went over to where the baby was in his little bassinet. He smiled and cooed, and she exclaimed as she brandished her long cigarette holder in a dramatic gesture, "Listen to that! He called me 'Aunt Virginia'!"

We will bless Brian eternally for that marvelous "coo" she so loosely interpreted.

We drove down the long driveway, out through those gates and onto the highway knowing in our hearts that God had given us favor with "Aunt Virginia" as He had given Joseph favor with Pharaoh! We were in seventh heaven . . . until we thought of our $27 in the bank and our three parishioners, Mr. and Mrs. Dysart and their little three-year-old daughter. We just had to believe that when God said, "Verily thou shalt inherit the land," He had some plan way beyond our own abilities to raise money.

The next step was to meet with Mrs. White and her attorney in about two weeks. That gave me time to try to raise some funds. I tried. *Oh, how I tried!* I approached friends and some wealthy people I knew. All I asked for was loans, not gifts. But though I tried so hard, I could raise no more than $20,000, and we had offered her $40,000. I dreaded going back to meet with Mr. Weisman and Mrs. White.

My fears were not unrealistic. From the beginning I could tell that her lawyer was very opposed to Mrs. White's selling to us.

"This is a ridiculous offer!" he fumed. "My client has been offered twice that amount by the Bishop. Who are you? What is the name of your denomination?" he demanded.

I had been through all that before with Mrs. White, but I slowly reiterated the long name.

"Never heard of them!" he retorted.

I made no further explanation. Mrs. White knew who we were. I left it there.

Before he could pry it out with his probing, I felt I had better reveal my bad news on my own initiative. I turned to Mrs. White, ignoring her lawyer completely. "Mrs. White, I cannot tell you how badly I feel about this. I was not trying to mislead you. I honestly thought I could raise $40,000, but I have been able to raise only $20,000."

Her response shocked me and nearly gave her Jewish lawyer a heart attack! "Well, perhaps I could just take the other $20,000 as a mortgage," she said without the slightest hesitation.

"How many people do you have?" her lawyer blurted out angrily.

No way was I going to let him know that we had only three persons plus ourselves. "Admittedly only a handful," I replied.

"Well, then, how in the name of heaven do you expect to be able to make the mortgage payments?" His question was quite valid. *But inadvertently he had included the proper answer!*

"Our people are tithers, Mr. Weisman," I said. "They give ten percent of their income to the Lord."

"I have never heard of such a thing!" he sputtered. "That's a lot to expect of your people."

"Mr. Weisman, you're a Jew. We got the idea from your people," I responded *very* firmly. "Your forefathers tithed because it was a Jewish law. We give out of love for the most wonderful Jew who ever lived, the Lord Jesus Christ."

He colored up and calmed down. "Well, if Mrs. White were to carry a mortgage, it would be at five and one-half percent, of course," he began.

"It would not!" Mrs. White interrupted, removing her long cigarette holder from her lips in order to speak, and gesturing emphatically with it. "It would be at five percent!"

He didn't argue with her, except with his dark, angry eyes.

The outcome of that afternoon's confrontation was that we came away from the Winnie Cha Estate knowing that soon we would be the owners of it—lock, stock and barrel (or should I say, antiques, Knabe baby grand piano, brand new Kelvinator Food-arama refrigerator, five-car garage, tennis courts, formal gardens and all?)! God had heard our believing prayer and the prayers of others we had enlisted to stand with us. He had moved upon the heart of the elegant, sophisticated, high-society Mrs. Winslow White, who had five servants. He had made her a *servant* of His that day. One day He would make her a *child* of His as well, when I would call upon her and her personal maid in their luxurious apartment just off Central Park in New York City.

The Winnie Cha Estate was ours now! Ever since it had been built, it had been God's to do with as He pleased. All things are!

Here's the Church: Where's the Steeple?

1957

*G*od had given us the Winnie Cha estate. It was really magnificent! The only thing it needed to make it look like a church to the people driving by was a steeple on the gabled wing that faced the road. I dreamed of having one someday. I put it on my prayer list.

A car drove up the long gravel driveway, mounting the hill on which the mansion stood. It swung around the circle in front of the main entrance and stopped in front of the pillared entry. I came down the circular staircase from our upstairs apartment. (We had taken five of the eleven bedrooms and made a spacious apartment out of them. The other six we had turned into classrooms for Sunday School.)

The couple at the front door were Frank and Lee Piazza. After introducing themselves they asked what we believed. "I am a Jehovah's Witness and my wife is a Roman Catholic," Frank said.

I responded by saying something that I regretted as soon as the words were out of my mouth. They seemed to me like such a poor choice of words: "Well, I'm afraid we don't believe as either of you do!"

They looked at each other, giving approving glances. I was not aware of what was going on until Frank spoke again. "You see, Lee will not allow me to take the children to Kingdom Hall and I will not allow her to raise the children Roman Catholic. So the children are growing up as atheists. We don't want that to happen. Last night we agreed that if we could find a place that didn't believe what either of us believed, we would take the children there!"

God had prompted me to say precisely the right thing, though it had seemed wrong to me at the moment.

They enrolled the children in our Sunday school and then thought they had better come with them for awhile to see what we were teaching them. It wasn't long before Lee gave her heart to Christ. I recall the first thing she said when she got up off her knees: "Now we must start praying for Frank!"

Frank took a little longer, but was also soundly converted after a few months. They became diligent workers in The Neighborhood Church of Commack. Frank was a carpenter. He built an exquisite parquet floor for the platform of our church (we used the main living room, seating ninety persons). One day I confided in him my desire to have a steeple to place on the peak of the roof facing the road. That would make the building look as if it had been originally built to be a church. He said he would gladly build it. I called a friend who was a structural engineer and told him what we wanted to do. I asked him to check the building to see if it would bear the weight.

He came to Winnie Cha. We went way back to the servant quarters where the staircase to the third floor attic was. As soon as we ascended into the attic, he said, "There is no way you could put a steeple up here. This structure is not capable of holding the weight."

"This is not the end I want it on," I reminded him as we walked toward the main center part of the building. As we climbed the three steps into this huge part of the attic, he commented, "These rafters are much better, but I would still be concerned. They should be reinforced."

I said, "This is not the wing on which I want it, either."

We descended a step or two into the wing facing the street.

He exclaimed, "You can build anything you want on top of these rafters! They are 2 x 10's on twelve-inch centers! They would hold a tremendous amount of weight."

When Mrs. White had added that wing to have an additional parlor on the first floor adjacent to the living room she never realized she was providing seating for an additional ninety persons. Nor did she know that the second floor which became her mammoth bedroom would one day be a huge living room in which Elaine and I would entertain up to fifty persons at a time. And I am sure she never dreamed that the unnecessarily strong rafters were being put in place to hold a steeple! *But God knew.* He had in fact planned it all in advance. She was just His "Cyrus," working as His servant though she had not yet known Him. I later had the joy of leading her to Christ before she passed away.

Frank built a graceful, slender spire. A crane lifted it into place, and the Winnie Cha mansion became, without question, the most impressive church in the area. It was perched high on the knoll above the highway, gracefully pointing its steeple, like a worshipful finger, toward the heavens.

Before They Shop, I Will Deliver

1958

*F*inances were extremely tight in the new Neighborhood Church of Commack. In fact, we had no salary at all for a long time, and then only $5 a week! But God was wonderfully faithful to our little family of three. Before we had moved there, He had given us a promise when we had wondered how we would eat, and especially if we could be sure of having food for little Brian, who was about one year old. The promise was so very specific: "Verily thou shalt be fed!"

One day Elaine made out her grocery list in preparation for a trip to the A&P market. It was *very* specific. We did not make impulse purchases. There was no room for that kind of thing in our lifestyle of those days.

Before she could go out the door, the doorbell rang. It was Doris Stondell, one of the ladies of our tiny congregation. She had in her arms two bags of groceries for us! We carried them up that grand circular staircase to our kitchen and unpacked them. In those bags were all the items on the grocery list, even to the very brands we would have selected from the shelves. God had sent Doris grocery shopping for us.

His promise is: "Before they call, I will answer."

Let's paraphrase that promise this way: "Before they shop, I will deliver their groceries."

God Knows "Perfectly Well"

1958

The registration renewal for our car was due in a few days, but Elaine and I had no money to pay the $12 fee. We were already having to trust God for grocery money each week. There simply wasn't any money for extras. We committed the need to the Lord and waited for His provision in answer to prayer. No answer was immediately forthcoming.

The final day came. We had to have those funds if we were to drive our car legally. That day the mail brought a gift of $12 from a friend. But that was not all; also enclosed in the envelope was a Motor Vehicle Department application to be filled out and submitted along with the fee! There was absolutely no question but that God had sent that money to meet that need.

> So don't worry at all about having enough food and clothing [and money to renew your car registration!] Why be like the heathen? For they . . . are deeply concerned about them. But your heavenly Father already knows *perfectly well* that you need them, and he will give them to you if you give him first place in your life and live as he wants you to. (Matthew 6:31-33, TLB, emphasis added)

Every little (and big) thing that concerns you, or that you have need of, is known "perfectly well" by your heavenly Father who delights to do for His children. Never forget that!

1958

When I attended Bible college in Nyack, New York, it was still a Bible institute from which we graduated in three years. After I became a pastor, I realized that I needed more formal education. By this time they were offering a B.S. degree, so I traveled back to Nyack a couple of times a week for a few years until I had earned my degree.

Then we opened the church in Commack, on Long Island. It was near a research center. Many of the new adherents were very well educated, holding master's degrees. This prompted me to go on for my master's as well, but I had no funds with which to pursue graduate work.

One day when I was visiting my alma mater, I happened to meet my friend, Dr. Harry Hardwick. He was a man I greatly admired. He enquired about my educational plans. I didn't realize he had a motive behind his questioning. He was soon to become the president of the St. Paul Bible College and he knew that he would eventually need to put together a team of his own choosing. I told him what I have told you.

He said, "Why don't you apply for a scholarship from New York University (NYU)? They have some scholarship funds available for a few graduate students."

I had never thought of that approach, having never been one to ask for things. I recalled immediately that my grades in undergraduate work had been good. Was it possible that I could even get a full semester's help toward a master of arts degree? What was there to lose other than the time to fill out an application form and the price of a stamp?

When the response finally arrived from NYU, I had thoroughly prepared myself to read, "We are sorry to inform you. . . ." To my amazement, I saw the following: "We have awarded you a tuition grant to cover all courses leading to a master of arts degree." That was more than twice what I had asked for! When God says that He will give to us the desires of our hearts, He means *every word* of that promise and often couples it with another that includes the words "above all that you ask or even think!"

Postscript: After getting my master of arts degree, Dr. Hardwick invited me to come to St. Paul Bible College in St. Paul, Minnesota to serve as his Dean of Men. Elaine and I moved there in 1960 with our two very small boys. I served for one year as the Dean of Men and then was made the Dean of Students. We lived in Minnesota for the next seventeen years, serving nine years at the college, followed by seven years with the Meadow Creek Church.

1961-1970

For you must teach others. . . . Teach these
great truths to trustworthy men who will,
in turn, pass them on to others.
(2 Timothy 2:2, TLB)

"If We Are Faithless..."

1961

Elaine and I were sitting reading in the living room of our first-floor apartment on the grounds of St. Paul Bible College. Our two sons, Brian and Gary, were both sleeping soundly in their room (we thought). They were very small boys.

Suddenly we heard the sound of little feet coming down the hallway to the living room, and there in the doorway appeared Gary, his face red and flushed, his eyes glazed. Elaine picked him up and held him on her lap. He felt like he was burning up. I went to get a thermometer to take his temperature.

It registered more than 105 degrees! We knew we had to pull that down quickly or he could have a convulsion, so we gave him some children's aspirin and bathed him in cool water. That did not help much. His temperature would not go below 103 degrees.

Suddenly the thought crossed my mind, "We haven't even prayed about this!" Immediately we had prayer for Gary and quickly noticed his temperature dropping. One hour later it was completely back to normal. We praised the Lord for His swift answer to our prayers.

The following day we took Gary to Sunday school at the Simpson Memorial Church. As we dropped him off, we told his Sunday school teacher how God had so wonderfully answered our prayer. Sunday night we put the children to bed and once again sat down to read in our living room.

Again we heard the patter of little feet in the hallway. There stood Gary. His face was red, his body was hot. We didn't need a thermometer to know that he was very ill. I did check, though, and found his temperature was almost as high as the night before. We reached for the aspirin bottle immediately and drew cool water for bathing him. Once again it had minimal effect.

Suddenly I looked over at Elaine sheepishly and said again, "We haven't even prayed about this!" We asked the Lord to forgive us for being so slow to learn and asked Him to do once again what He had done the night before. He did! Within an hour his temperature was completely normal.

The next afternoon at the faculty coffee break, I gave a testimony to those at my table about what the Lord had done the two nights before. Then "Job's comforters" started talking. One said, "Oh, that sounds like rheumatic fever to me. The temperature comes and goes fairly rapidly."

Rheumatic fever! Oh, no!

Another chimed in, "That sounds more like mononucleosis to me. It has a fluctuating temperature like that."

Mono! I knew how devastating that could be.

At the supper table I told Elaine what they had said. I forgot that "little heads have big ears." I probably should not have been saying it in front of Brian.

He looked up from his eating and said to me, "Daddy, is Gary going to be sick again tonight?"

With all my heart I wanted to be able to say by faith, "No, Brian, Gary is not going to have a fever tonight!" I just couldn't muster up enough faith to be able to make that statement confidently. Instead I said, "Why don't we go have prayer for him right now." The four of us left the table and went into the living room and knelt together by the couch. I don't remember what the rest of us prayed, but I remember vividly what little Gary said: "Thank You, Jesus, that I am not going to get hot tonight!" That little prayer of faith was so definite and so positive. It must have been very pleasing to God.

That night Elaine and I sat reading in the living room again, feeling deeply pleased that there was no squeak of the bedroom door and no patter of little feet in the hallway. When it was time to go to bed, just before going into our own bedroom, I slipped quietly into the boys' bedroom across the hallway. I leaned over Gary's crib and put my hand on his brow. It was cool and I knew he was perfectly all right, in answer to prayer. I rejoiced.

On my way back to our own bedroom, the Lord spoke to my heart so definitely: "Why did you put your hand on his brow?"

I knew the answer immediately—unbelief! I suddenly saw how offensive our unbelief is to God. If it were not for His grace and character, I doubt that we would ever receive anything from Him! "If we believe not, yet he abideth faithful: he cannot deny himself" (2 Timothy 2:13, KJV). "[I]f we are faithless, he will remain faithful, for he cannot disown himself" (2 Timothy 2:13, NIV). It is upon God's unchanging, gracious nature that we must depend.

The Gilliland Family

1961

There is one special leading of the Lord in my lifetime that thrills me as much as, or more, than any other. It happened during a youth camp where I was the evangelist. When I preach a salvation sermon, I sometimes make the point that a person must be born into *God's* family by spiritual birth, saying something like this: "*Physical* birth brought you into the *Smith* family, the *Jones* family, the *Johnson* family. But it takes a *spiritual* birth to bring you into *God's* family." That truth is based upon the third chapter of John's Gospel. As often as I can, I make that third name one that is familiar in the congregation, or at least typical of the area. If there is a strong ethnic group represented in that church I often choose a name that is obviously of that ethnicity, like "Friesen" in a Mennonite area, or "Swensen" in a Scandinavian area.

At Rivercrest Bible Camp in Fremont, Nebraska, I was preaching one night and heard myself say those familiar words, but the final name on that list was *not* a familiar one! On the contrary, it was quite a tongue twister! "The Gilliland family," I said!

I remember thinking to myself right while preaching, *What an unusual name to include! Somewhere I have heard it before, but it is difficult to say that name, let alone to remember it!* (Actually, I realized later, I had seen the name "Gilliland" months before on an application form that had crossed my desk at the St. Paul Bible College.)

When I gave the invitation, there was a young lady who came to the altar crying. I prayed with her. She said, "Oh, pastor, when you included 'the Gilliland family,' I knew that God was speaking to *me*. My name is Wanda Gilliland!"

God had chosen to slip an unusual, unfamiliar name into my mouth, to achieve His wonderful purposes. I wish this were the norm, rather than the exception!

The Joy of Having to Trust

1961

When we moved to St. Paul Bible College in Minnesota from Commack, Long Island, we had a salary again for the first time in a long time. In some ways it was wonderful, even though the monthly paycheck was not very large. At least we could budget and live within it, knowing how much money we had available. But we did miss having to trust God. One day I expressed that to Elaine.

To my surprise, she acknowledged feeling the same way.

"Let's ask God to put us in a position (not of our own doing) where we will have to trust Him again," I suggested.

She agreed.

We began to pray that way. *What a scary thing to do!* Almost immediately our older car broke down and when I checked on the price of repairs I found it was not worth the cost. We went to see Don Greenberg who owned the American Motors dealership in a small town north of the Bible college. He had a very nice station wagon that would serve our family well. Don was a deeply committed Christian who regularly assisted Christian workers by cutting his profit margin drastically. He offered that wagon to us for a most reasonable price.

We sat down and examined our finances, trying to figure out where we could find the funds to buy it without borrowing. Pulling everything together that we possibly could, we still came up $135 short.

Suddenly I remembered our prayer! "Honey! This is what we have been asking God to do. This is our opportunity to trust Him again for our finances," I said with excitement. We prayed together about the car we wanted (and needed), asking God to provide the $135 shortfall.

It was evening. I didn't usually go to my office during the evening hours, but I had forgotten something. I headed across campus—we lived on one edge of the campus—toward the administration building. I entered a back door, cut through the main lounge and started to pass the mailboxes and switchboard en route to my office.

As I neared the mailboxes I automatically glanced toward my own box, knowing, of course, that there would be nothing in it. It was just the force of habit. Through the glass window I saw an envelope! I spun the dials using my memorized combination, opened the little door, took the piece of mail out and carried it to my office.

It was from the Minnesota Sunday School Association. Some weeks earlier I had given the devotions each morning while their large convention was in progress. I honestly didn't remember the fact that they had not given me an honorarium. When I opened the envelope I found a check for $135 along with their nice note of appreciation. I could hardly wait to get back to our apartment to share the exciting news of how God had so quickly responded to our need.

Yes, there was most certainly a special joy in having to trust again!

What Are the Odds?

1963

Our little family of four was hurrying along the Ohio Turnpike en route to Gramma and Grampa Shepson's and Gramma and Grampa Campbell's homes. The boys were excited about seeing their four grandparents and, of course, we were also looking forward to seeing our parents. The car was a used one with a lot of miles on it; however, it was functioning quite well on this trip. Then it happened!

As we pulled into one of the turnpike service areas, I was about to shut off the motor when it sputtered, coughed and died! I didn't have to turn the key to stop the motor. What an awful feeling I had in the pit of my stomach. Even though there would be help right there in the service area, I knew how much they charged their customers. They had them right where they wanted them. There was no other place to go for help.

We asked the Lord to give us wisdom as to what to do. I am *not* a mechanic. I know next to nothing about cars. I tried to restart the motor, but the battery was weak and would barely turn the starter. I lifted the hood.

Just then another car pulled into the spot next to us, on the side of our car where the battery was. I heard someone call my name!

"Mr. Shepson, do you need some help?" It was Judy Pata, one of the girls from St. Paul Bible College where

I taught, which at this point was nearly 1,000 miles away! She had jumper cables in her car, and very quickly the motor was going again and we were able to go on to Gramma and Grampa Campbell's house without further difficulty, and Grampa Campbell was an automobile mechanic!

"I Apologize, Ma'am!"

1964

I was deeply provoked with him, yet underneath it all I knew how much I loved this vivacious, young, indefatigable boy from Florida. His mother had put up with his excess energy for all those eighteen years. Now it was *my* turn.

He enjoyed swimming in the tropical swamps among the cypress trees and was in his glory when he could catch some of the wildlife. Once his mother came home from shopping, opened her refrigerator door and screamed! There was a live baby alligator staring at her. Her fearless son meant no harm; he just wanted the reptile's metabolism to slow down a bit so he could control him better. On another occasion she discovered that he had put a larger alligator up on the roof for safekeeping.

Now, at St. Paul Bible College, he was repeatedly getting into mischief. There wasn't anything mean or destructive about him. After all, what harm did it do to place a Volkswagen in the library window, as if it were the showroom of a dealership? These were college pranks and with some of them, I simply looked the other way.

But there were others that had an element of danger in them that I could not, as the Dean of Students, conscientiously overlook. Take, for example, the tying of a dead deer to the flagpole chain and then enlisting a group of fellows to help him hoist it to the top, so it would hang there like a flag. *No harm in that!*

Well, at least he *thought* there wouldn't be, until the chain broke and the deer hurtled down from the sky, landing on the shoulder of one of his "accomplices in crime," sending him to the emergency room with a dislocated collarbone.

Then there was the time when the college nurse phoned me with a tone of desperation in her voice. "Come quickly," she urged. "I need help to get him to the hospital. He was playing basketball with some of the fellows in the men's lounge, and the ball went right through a pane of the glass doors into the dining hall with his arm right after it. He cut it badly, and as he pulled it back through, it was cut some more by the jagged glass. I need to wrap the arm in towels. I will squeeze his lower arm and I need you to squeeze his upper arm while we transport him to the hospital."

I hurried over to the dorm, and was with him as he went into surgery. It took ninety-two stitches in order to repair the damage to that arm.

En route to the hospital he said, "Oh, this is nothing, you should have seen when I did this!" He pulled up his pant leg to show me scars from some other escapade!

How do you solve a problem like this Virgil? I asked myself, substituting his name in that catchy tune from "The Sound of Music." Again I sat with him in my office. He was all dressed up so nicely. He always showered and wore his Sunday best as if he were going to church when he had to appear before me! He smelled nice from the aftershave lotion he had splashed on.

In keeping with his best southern upbringing, he was apologizing profusely for another prank, "Sorry, sir. Didn't mean any harm by it, sir. I promise it will never happen again, sir. I apologize, ma'am!"

Ma'am? He was so nervous that he threw in a "Ma'am" and never even recognized his error.

That almost always happened. I suppressed a smile.

Then came a rapid change of emotions in me. Suddenly I was overwhelmed with the hopelessness of calling him into my office to try to explain that pranks that have danger associated with them, either to himself or to others, I would not tolerate. Here sat a young man with all kinds of boundless energy but he was using it in the wrong way.

"Virgil Adams!" I said with tears in my eyes, "You have energy plus and you are using it in the wrong way! With your kind of stamina you would make a terrific missionary out in New Guinea hiking those impossible trails and reaching those almost unreachable tribal people. You remind me of Tom Bozeman, a missionary who serves faithfully out there. You have his kind of energy, but you don't know what to do with it. If you would get your act together, you could be used of the Lord just as he is!"

It was Virgil's eyes that filled with tears now as he arose to leave. With one more apology, he excused himself. He was too choked up to talk just then.

Later, when he had his emotions under control, he came back to my office to say, "Mr. Shepson, you didn't know it, but Tom Bozeman has been my hero since I was a small boy. I know him well. When you said I remind you of him and that I have what it takes to do what he is doing, well, I just think maybe God is calling me to be a missionary, and I would love to go to New Guinea."

It was at a missionary meeting where I showed slides of the Dani and Uhunduni (Damal) tribal work that Bonnie Scott came to the altar to commit her life to missionary service, perhaps even there in New Guinea. Bonnie was reserved and quiet and thin. She was almost frail. In no way did she seem to be a match for the bundle of energy Mr. and Mrs. Adams had produced named "Virgil," yet the Lord directed them together. Not only did I have the pleasure of marrying them, but also my son, Brian, was the little ring bearer! It was an exciting day in Simpson Memorial Church in St. Paul, Minnesota.

Virgil and Bonnie went out to New Guinea (now called Irian Jaya) and served many terms there before finally coming home because of Bonnie's health. They and their four wonderful boys settled at Toccoa Falls College where they serve at the time of this writing. You would never guess what Virgil's position is. He is the Dean of Men! At least they won't be able to put anything over on him; *he knows all the tricks!*

The vivacious, energetic, full-of-pranks Virgil Adams did indeed "get his act together" and God has greatly used him as a result. He is in demand as a missionary speaker. He can tell about some fantastic adventures, as well as results among those primitive people in "the land that time forgot."

Anthropology—The Study of Man?

1964

I wanted a Ph.D., not for my own sake, but for the sake of St. Paul Bible College where I was teaching. They paid my tuition in graduate school; I did the work.

I guess the thing I disliked the most about the University of Minnesota was the lack of available parking. Frequently I had to park ten blocks or more from Ford Hall where my class in anthropology met regularly.

I dashed from the stale air of the classroom and hurried across bustling University Avenue. The day was full of responsibilities back at the Bible college and I was glad to be out from under Dr. Spencer's sarcastic, even sometimes blasphemous remarks. The quarter was nearly finished now. I wouldn't have to endure that atheist's degrading remarks about believers much longer.

I headed back toward my car and ultimately my own desk, back at the college. Following the crowd of students toward the edge of the campus, I hurriedly walked a half dozen blocks, before I suddenly realized with disgust that I had left my notebook back in the classroom. What a sense of deep frustration! Just when I was in a great hurry, I had made things even worse by my carelessness.

I spun on my heel and headed back toward Ford Hall. Inwardly I was fuming over that round trip involving twelve or more blocks of unnecessary delay. "Talk about an absent-minded professor!" I mumbled to myself.

I rushed up to University Avenue and arrived there just as the light turned so I could not cross. "Even the lights are against me!" I grumbled.

Suddenly the thought struck me, *Does the forgetting of my notebook and the turning of the traffic light fit into God's blanket statement that "everything happens for our good"* (Romans 8:28, author paraphrase)? In my heart I knew His promise applied even then, so I tried to relax.

As I waited, a young man came from behind and stood beside me at the crossing. The light turned green, and we started to cross together.

"Are you a preacher?" he asked suddenly.

"Why, yes! But how did you know that?" I wondered aloud.

"I noticed that one day you had a book by Billy Graham among your books in class," he said. "I am in Dr. Spencer's anthropology class along with you."

He stopped and we chatted briefly, then he turned to go another direction.

"Wait a minute!" I called after him, realizing that God might have brought me back to that corner for a very specific purpose. "Are you a Christian?" I asked him.

"No, I don't believe that kind of thing anymore," he said. "I used to. I was brought up in a Baptist church and I know all about those teachings, but since I have come to the university I have rejected them. Of course, my mother still believes those things. In fact, she prays for me every day!"

I stood talking with him awhile, and before we parted, I said, "Bob, let me tell you how we happened to be standing there together waiting for that light to turn green." I told him the story. "I think God cares about you very much, Bob. He hears those prayers of your Christian mother, too. I am just simple enough to believe that He is the One who arranged for me to forget my notebook and even to be caught by the red light so you would come and stand right beside me and we would have this conversation. God has not forgotten you, and He won't!"

With that, we parted. I never had another encounter with him. I am hopeful that the one we did have was planned by God as a part of His strategy to make that young man realize that even though he had rejected God, God had not forgotten about him. I'd like to have Bob be the one to introduce me to his mother when I meet her in heaven!

1964

_I_ was late arriving at the service that night during spiritual emphasis week at St. Paul Bible College, due to counseling with one of the students. I found a seat on the aisle near the rear of the narrow auditorium. Many of the students were stirred by the speaker's message and went to the altar to pray when the invitation was extended. I normally went down to pray with some of them. I felt it was important for faculty members to be in those services, ready to assist at the altar.

That night, however, I stayed in my seat because I had a concern for a big football-player-type fellow across the aisle from me and up one row. It appeared to me that he was struggling emotionally.

After praying awhile for him, I finally crossed the aisle and laid my hand on his shoulder. "Would you like to talk, Gary?" I asked.

"Yes, Mr. Shepson. May we go to your office?"

"Surely!" I said. I couldn't care less whether he met God at the altar or in my office, just so he met the Lord.

In the privacy of my office Gary told me the story of his childhood. His father had abandoned his mother when he was a small boy, leaving her to raise him and his sister all alone. She had done a good job, Gary insisted, but still he had longed for the attention of his dad. "Mr.

Shepson, he lived in the same town with us, but he never contacted us! I became a star football player on our high school team, and one day my picture was in the newspaper as big as life, because I had made the winning touchdown. *Now*, I thought to myself, *Dad will call me or drop me a note to say he is proud of me.* But, Mr. Shepson, he never did. *He never did!*" He put his head on his arms on the edge of my desk and sobbed.

When he finished crying, I said, "Gary, I would like to show you some Scripture verses." I turned to the Psalms and read to him, "When my father and my mother forsake me, then the LORD will take me up" (Psalm 27:10, KJV).

"I never knew the Bible said that!" he exclaimed.

"Well it does, Gary, and listen to this." I read to him, "A father to the fatherless, a defender of widows, is God . . . " (68:5).

Once again, he was thrilled to learn that the Bible addressed his specific needs. After I had prayed with him, Gary asked me if I would write those references down for him.

I gave him those and a couple of others that were similar.

He left my office clutching the paper and thanking me for showing them to him. Suddenly he spun on his heel and looked me straight in the eye. "Mr. Shepson," he asked abruptly, "why do *you* have those verses underlined in *your* Bible?"

I wasn't ready to be transparent, not then. My father had come back to my mother for their final years together. I didn't want to talk about the years of separation when God had used those verses to comfort me.

Thinking as quickly as I could, I replied, "Maybe it was for you, Gary. Maybe it was for you."

Satisfied, he walked away and I closed my office door, but I did not return to my desk. I stood right where I was, thinking. Ringing in my ears were my own words, "Maybe it was for you!" For the first time I came to the realization that God *had* allowed the heartaches of my childhood so that I would be able to minister to Gary Bowden and to a multitude of other fatherless boys and girls when I became a man.

Now whenever I share these verses—Psalm 27:10, 68:5, 146:9, Deuteronomy 10:18, Hosea 14:3 and Psalm 10:14, 18—with some boy or girl who missed so much because there was no faithful dad in the home, I remember my own words played back hundreds of times through the years: "Maybe it was for you!"

A Double Miracle

1965

*T*he rickety, top-heavy truck-turned-bus careened around curves boasting hair-raising drop-offs with no guardrails. I would have been terribly frightened even if I had been alone, but in addition to my own welfare, I was concerned for the lives of the young people from St. Paul Bible College who were traveling with me there in Ecuador, South America. I felt *very* responsible for them.

The driver was either reckless or drunk, perhaps both. There seemed to be altogether too much play in the steering wheel. He was frequently trying to bring the bus back to our own side of the road or away from another precipice. I was greatly relieved when the road from Riobamba to Quito straightened out and leveled off, and there were no more drop-offs. The worst stretch of road was behind us.

What I did not realize was that in some ways we were now on the most dangerous part of the trip. The lack of a challenge lulled the driver into a stupefied sleep more than once. A couple of times I actually reached over and put my hand on his slumping shoulder to awaken him. With a quick jerk of his drooping head, he came alive in time to bring the bus back on course.

Three of the six of us were sitting on front seats either behind the driver or across the aisle from him.

The other three were directly behind in the second row of seats. The bus was packed, yet quietness prevailed. The Quichua Indians are a quiet people. Even the chickens were docile, yet there was an air of apprehension because neither the Indians nor we gringos were placing any confidence in this obviously unqualified "chofer." I was too busy watching the road to enjoy the magnificent, snow-capped Cotopaxi Mountain which towered above us to the right.

I reached over again to touch the driver's arm and get his eyelids open. Then it happened! With not a single curve in sight, nor a horrendous drop-off to worry us, nor even any oncoming traffic to be a concern, our driver drifted off into sleep once again. He awakened with a start as the bus crossed the median line. He pulled it back sharply, too sharply.

We headed for the ditch on the right side of the road.

He jerked the wheel hard to the left and once again we headed across the median at a rakish angle. He pulled with all his might to the right, but it was no use. The top-heavy bus was already tipping over. There was no stopping it now. Before the horrified passengers could even muster their screams, the ancient bus was on its right side, skidding noisily across the irregular pavement, making metallic screeches and screams of its own. It hurtled across the sewage ditch at the side of the road and punched a huge hole in the wall of an adobe house that squatted at the edge of the road.

There was broken glass everywhere. Chickens were running around squawking out their panic. Some of the passengers were softly moaning. The little Indian boy on the bottom of the heap of our row had a broken leg. I was being drenched by liquid that was pouring on me from above. I realized from the pungent odor that it was fuel that was soaking my clothing.

If this wreck catches on fire, I've had it! I realized to my horror. I staggered to my feet and started walking around, like the others were doing. We were walking on the shards of broken glass that had been the windows on the right side of the bus. There was no way out! Both exits were on the right side of the vehicle and that was the side resting against the ground. I glanced at each of my students. Dale was OK. Dan and his brother, Dean, both appeared to be dazed but all right. Larry and Connie, his wife, were badly shaken, but they were up and walking around.

Since I was the only one drenched with fuel, I felt I had to get out of there quickly, somehow. I would feel so much safer out in the open with the air evaporating the highly combustible fuel from my clothing.

Men were climbing up on top of the extra wide bus, reaching strong arms down through those broken windows and pulling the traumatized passengers up to safety. I knew that with my fused spine and lack of flexibility, that would be a very difficult way for me to make my exit. I noticed that the front door was open, but it opened into a ditch that had filthy water in it. I decided to crawl out through that putrid water. I breathed a sigh of relief when I was out of the danger of fire, away from that hot, hissing engine.

One by one the bruised, bleeding, broken passengers were pulled up and out of the bus through those top windows. Connie's back had been badly wrenched, but she was walking around stiffly. Dale Groeneweg dropped nimbly down to the hood of the motor and then on down to the ground. Dan and Dean Dainsberg were pulled out next and they too appeared OK as they were helped down to the cab area and then on to the ground. But then Dan turned the other way, and I saw blood covering that side of his face and dripping off his chin. He was bleeding profusely!

I immediately applied pressure with my thumb on the pressure point on Dan's jaw that controlled the flow of blood to that side of his head. I told the students to gather up our scattered baggage that had been on top the bus. We huddled in the middle of the road, far from Quito and far from the medical help Dan needed.

I tried to flag down vehicles with my free right hand, but no one would stop to help us. No one wanted to get involved. We desperately needed to get to the HCJB hospital, but in Ecuador people avoid involvement like the plague. To stop is tantamount to admitting that in some way you have *caused* the accident!

Lord Jesus, my heart cried out, *I* must have help! *I ask You to have the next car stop for us,* and *I ask that the driver will be able to speak English. I cannot wrestle with my meager knowledge of the Spanish language at a time like this.* I knew the answer to that bold prayer would necessitate a *double* miracle!

The next vehicle was a large station wagon. I tried to flag it down, realizing that only God could make it stop; He did. The driver rolled down his window and enquired in beautiful English, "May I help you?"

My heart shouted praises. I responded, "Yes, please, I need to get this boy to the Vozandes Hospital as quickly as possible."

"I know right where that is. Get in!" he said.

We sped toward Quito and the HCJB Hospital. Dan, somewhat faint and limp, was sitting beside me, cradled in my left arm. One of the fingers of my right hand was pressing on the niche in his jawbone to stop the flow of blood. As we sped along toward the hospital, I could not help praising God with tears for sending a station wagon with a Harvard educated Ecuadorian at the wheel who knew right where the Vozandes Hospital was located.

Dan Dainsberg can show you the scar in his eyebrow where the doctor put the stitches, but he is not defaced. All our lives both Dan and I will praise the God who controls languages, vehicles and all circumstances; the God who, according to His own claim, orders our very footsteps. "[C]all upon me in the day of trouble; I will deliver you, and you will honor me" is His promise (Psalm 50:15). How quickly He responded with the double miracle we needed that nightmarish day on the road from Riobamba!

Transition

1968-1970

*O*ur years at St. Paul Bible College were very happy ones. We had the privilege of helping to train hundreds of sincere Christian young men and women for the Lord's service.

Toward the end of the 1960s, I was invited to preach for a vibrant group of sincere people who were starting a new independent church in Anoka, Minnesota. I ministered there Sundays for a year or more and kept urging the congregation to call a permanent pastor, because an ever increasing number were attending. They delayed and delayed. The grade school cafeteria became too small for us, so we moved into one-half of the gymnasium. That became too small, so we rented the entire gymnasium of Crooked Lake Elementary School. That was becoming too small as well, so we were pleased when we were given land.

Almost immediately we began to build. This was to be the first of six building projects in the next seven years, but I could not have known that. Nor could I foresee that the little group of believers would grow to more than 500 during our time with them. I believe they are over 1,000 now, as I write this.

We continued to urge them to get a permanent, full-time pastor. Finally they insisted that they felt certain *we* were to come to serve them full-time. It took a while for us to become aware that this was God's will for us and not just the will of the people. God, through my devotional reading, made that unmistakably clear. We accepted the call. Our son, Brian, was entering junior high. Our second son, Gary, was still in grade school. We built an elegant five-bedroom parsonage by the lake, moved into it and for the next eight years lived there and pastored the Meadow Creek Baptist Church of Anoka, Minnesota. ("Baptist" was dropped from the name a few years later.)

1972-1979

*I'm going to do a brand new thing.
See, I have already begun!
(Isaiah 43:19, TLB)*

Divine Bookkeeping

1972

*T*he basement auditorium we had built in Anoka, Minnesota had rapidly become too small for our growing congregation. There were only three Sunday school rooms off to the side of it, and we desperately needed more. The embryonic Meadow Creek Church was few in number, but big in faith and youthful enthusiasm. I brought the board a sketch of a basement addition with an estimated price of $22,500. It would provide a small assembly room flanked by a cluster of classrooms and two more rest rooms.

The board liked the plan but had some valid objections. "If we go any further into debt, we may never get above ground with our building," someone said. The plan had been to build a sanctuary above the current basement structure, but that would give us no additional space for Christian education.

"Why don't we build this proposed basement addition debt-free?" I suggested.

You could almost sense the incredulity of the men, without their expressing it. Someone did say, "Pastor, we don't have that kind of money!"

"Does God?" I asked. "Why don't we think and pray about it for a week and then discuss it further. I believe God could enable us to erect that building debt-free."

A week later we met again. To our surprise, we discovered that the Lord had given us a nearly unanimous opinion about it! We would dare to trust God. There would be no big push for funds. We would just let the people know that we planned to believe God for a miracle on Thanksgiving Eve, when we would receive a special faith offering aimed toward the debt-free construction of the addition.

Excitement began to build, especially when someone announced that he and his wife were giving up a planned vacation and contributing those funds. Another said that he didn't really need the new snowmobile he had been saving for and he was planning to put that money in the offering. Others confided sacrificial plans that I shared with the congregation without naming those special donors. The thrill of expectation was growing by the day.

Thanksgiving Eve we had a dinner together and following that we planned to receive the offering. I told the men I wanted the people to be given plain white envelopes in which to place their offering. They would be told to write the amount (not their name) on the outside of the envelope so I could read the figures aloud. We would all tabulate them on our paper tablecloths and rejoice together as the total climbed. At each plateau, we would stop to sing praises to the Lord.

"Oh, no! Not that way, Pastor!" Harold Kinghorn pleaded. "You see, Pastor, some of us who count the offering are planning to add to it to make up the deficit if we come up a little short!"

"No," I insisted, "let's trust the Lord and not man."

As the total climbed higher and higher, we rejoiced together with songs of praise. When we reached the final total of $22,507, you would have thought we had gone off the deep end! We clapped and shouted and laughed and shed tears of joy. We had asked God for $22,500, which was an "impossible" sum for our little group. He had given that exact amount plus seven *which is the number of perfection!*

There were also two pledges made that we did not include in the total, since we had stipulated that the offering had to be cash. One was for $2,500 promised by a couple who were trying to sell their home. "When it is sold," they wrote, "we will contribute the money." The other pledge was for $1,500 from someone who wrote, "I am expecting an inheritance soon. When it comes, I will give $1,500."

When the basement addition was completed, there was a cost override of exactly $4,000, and by that time both pledges—totaling $4,000—had been paid in full. God knew we needed $26,500 and not the $22,500 we had estimated and He provided for that as well, in a most amazing manner. The perfection of divine bookkeeping can never be denied.

Will God Help an Overweight Problem?

1974

I was so excited! Of all the mission fields where I had ministered, this was the one I would most enjoy returning to. The Meadow Creek Church was paying my way to go out to New Guinea (later renamed Irian Jaya) to minister to the Alliance missionaries at their field conference. I wrote ahead to ask if there were things they would like me to bring. The list was long! It was a privilege to take them the things they could not get out there in that primitive part of the world.

When Elaine took me to the Minneapolis airport I knew my baggage was somewhat overweight, but I was shocked to discover exactly how much—ninety-four pounds!

The agent told me it would be $250 for the excess baggage.

I told him that I could not afford that, and that I was so disappointed for these were things for the missionaries.

He very kindly said, "I'll tell you what I can do. I cannot do anything for Pan American, but for Northwest Airlines, I can check you as far as Los Angeles. You will have to pick up your bags there and recheck them with Pan Am. I don't know what they will do for you."

"Wonderful!" I said. "And, thank you so very much." I turned to Elaine and said, "Honey, I will be changing planes in California while the evening service is in progress. Ask the church people to pray earnestly. God can give me favor with the agent there just as He did with the one here."

In California I waited and waited for those bags to come down the baggage chute. Everyone else's luggage had come, but not mine. Mine were the very last ones to slide down the ramp to the carousel. It was frustrating, as I didn't have much time to get from Northwest to Pan Am. The connection was tight, and I was uptight!

The Pan Am terminal from which the plane would depart for Fiji was on the opposite arm of the big horseshoe-shaped airport road. The center of the horseshoe was all parking area. I put the baggage on a rented cart and started across that parking lot, but halfway across I encountered a big fence! I had to retrace my steps, pulling that heavily loaded cart and then go all the way around the giant horseshoe to Pan Am's terminal. Departure time was getting closer and closer.

There were a half dozen agents at Pan Am. I prayed the Lord would help me get in the right line, the one that would move the fastest. He answered the first half of that prayer, but not the last half! My line was painfully slow; all the others moved faster. With only fifteen minutes left until departure, there were still a half dozen people in line ahead of me. I groaned. I was *terribly* nervous.

The agent looked at his watch. He looked at the long lines, and then he shouted, "Is there anyone in line for the flight to Fiji?"

I shot my hand up.

"Get up here!" he commanded. "You will miss the plane!"

I dragged my bags up front. He quickly filled out tags for them, and without even weighing them, threw them on the belt and ordered me to run for the gate!

God had answered prayer for the next long leg of the flight.

For the final leg on Garuda Airlines, God brought along Karl Franklin, who was the head of the Wycliffe Center at Ukarumpa. He heard of my overweight plight and said, "I have only my briefcase. Let me check a couple of your bags on my ticket."

Only on one short leg of the trip did I have to pay anything. The fee was only $23, which was less than ten percent of the $250 they had wanted back in Minneapolis. Oh yes, God certainly can take care of overweight problems . . . of *any* kind!

The Timely Resurrection
of an Old Habit

1974

I knew my mother was right when she scolded me during my childhood years for drinking out of the pitcher instead of pouring some into a glass and drinking from that. The habit didn't die easily, but with stern scoldings and consistent discipline, it faded away completely.

When I traveled to New Guinea to minister at the field conference I was given a room in a very plain, rustic, motel-type structure. It was at the edge of the compound near the chapel at Pyramid in the primitive Baleim Valley.

Ministering to the missionaries in that exotic culture was a fabulous experience. I loved the Dani and Uhunduni tribal people. The only problem was that I developed a very severe cold. Fortunately a missionary doctor was on the grounds giving the missionaries their annual physicals. Dr. Robb White took good care of me, too, regularly monitoring my lungs for pneumonia. He gave me some prescription-strength pills to take at set intervals, even in the middle of the night.

There was no electricity, and there was no moon to compensate. Only in my memory was the layout of the room stored! I groped my way cautiously over to the table where the bottle of pills, the pitcher of water with the lid on it and the empty glass were. I fumbled around and found the pill bottle. By intense concentration I managed to get one out without spilling any. I put the pill in my mouth. Then I lifted the pitcher to pour some water into the glass, putting the lip of the pitcher on the rim of the glass.

Suddenly I had the strongest urge to repeat my childhood habit! No one was there to see me.

In fact, in the pitch darkness of that crude little room, no one could have seen me even if he had been right there with me! Feeling a bit sheepish, I lifted the pitcher to my mouth and took a swig, swallowing the pill with a noisy gulp that challenged the night sounds of the jungle. I felt a slight twinge of guilt as I reflected upon my childhood training.

In the morning when I saw the glass into which I had nearly poured that water, I realized that the strong urge was not simply the resurgence of a childhood pattern, but was the prompting of a watchful angel. There, crawling around in that empty glass, was one of the ugliest bugs I had ever seen in my whole life! In the darkness I could have swallowed that grotesque thing along with the pill, but for the graciousness of my watchful, caring Lord! Sometimes I think I should write my own paraphrase of the Scriptures (just for myself). It would include such a rendition as this: "For he will command his angels concerning you to guard you in all your ways. They will encourage you to drink out of a covered pitcher so you will not swallow a hideous beetle" (Psalm 91:11, CWS).

Can These Bones Live?

1975

*P*astor! *My wife is dead!* She is lying on the floor by her chair and my daughter is trying to give her CPR. We have sent for the ambulance." Rex Camp's voice was strange, almost mechanical, but still I recognized him.

"I'll meet you in emergency at Mercy Hospital!" I assured him and raced for my car.

The wailing ambulance arrived there first. When I came in, just minutes after the Camp family arrived with their "dead-on-arrival" wife and mother, I noted that the doctors were working over her feverishly, attempting to shock her heart back into action. Her daughter was close to hysteria.

The doctor called me aside. "Pastor, I have gotten her heart beating temporarily again, and she is breathing with the aid of a breathing machine, but there is no hope. She was too long without oxygen to the brain. She will not live. There is not one chance in 10,000 that this woman will ever open her eyes again, and even then, if she did, she would know nothing. Because of how traumatized the family is, I will try to keep her 'alive' artificially overnight. In the morning I will remove the machines and let her go. Please do what you can to prepare the family for tomorrow. Not telling them all this tonight will give them some time to adjust to the inevitable."

The family and I stayed in the intensive care waiting room until midnight. Every hour they let the family in for five minutes. At midnight, knowing what they would face in the morning, I urged them to go home and get some rest. I volunteered to stay with her. "They will even allow me to go into intensive care with her. I can sit right there in her room until you come back in the morning," I assured them. They finally agreed.

After they left, Mrs. Camp's condition deteriorated. Her heart went into fibrillation. Gail, the nurse, summoned all kinds of help with her "Code Blue" alarm. I stood back against the wall and watched, almost horrified, as they swiftly attached the paddles to her chest and the doctor called for the powerful surge of electricity. Her body literally leaped upward. I had never seen that except on television. It worked! Her heart stabilized. The fibrillation ceased.

An hour or so later, I was alone in the room with her and I noted on the heart-monitor that her heartbeat was climbing steadily. It seemed in my unprofessional opinion to be becoming dangerously high. I was almost ready to call Gail, when the alarm sounded. Once again a team raced into highly concentrated action. They attempted to shock her heart out of fibrillation again. The first attempt was not successful. The second one, using a higher voltage, succeeded. The doctor glanced toward me and shook his head. I knew what he was thinking.

After awhile, Gail left the room again, and I was alone with Mrs. Camp. *Lord*, I prayed, as I stood by her bedside, *I believe in divine healing. You are able. You could restore Mrs. Camp completely, even though that heart specialist said, "There is not one chance in 10,000." Please do it! Please prove that You are Jehovah-Rapha. Please let Mrs. Camp open her eyes and even know me!*

Suddenly, Mrs. Camp's eyelids fluttered and then opened. I rang for the nurse.

As Gail entered the room, she heard me saying, "This is Pastor Shepson, Mrs. Camp. Do you know me?"

She nodded her head, "Yes."

"Are you in any pain?"

She indicated by a shake of her head that she was not.

I said to Gail in amazement, "This is most encouraging!"

Gail exclaimed, "Pastor Shepson, this is a miracle!"

Then Mrs. Camp slipped back into unconsciousness.

Lord, I began praying, *You have already worked one miracle; now please let her begin to breathe on her own!* I don't know how long I prayed that way, but I do remember vividly the first time the yellow light came on indicating that she had taken that one breath without any assistance from the breathing machine.

My heart rejoiced!

Ten minutes later she took another breath, and then another and another. By morning she was breathing on her own and able to greet her thrilled family. Three weeks later Elaine and I sat in her kitchen enjoying a delicious piece of cherry pie she had baked for us.

"Not one chance in 10,000!" the doctor had said, but the God who can make even dead bones come alive, surely can restore dead bodies, too. He did it with Lazarus, didn't He?

To Move or Not to Move

1977

*I*nvitations to move away from Anoka, Minnesota came somewhat regularly. For the most part it was easy to say, "Thank you, but no thank you." We loved it where we were at the Meadow Creek Church. We loved the people and they loved us. Then a very aggressive church with terrific potential approached us. We did not feel completely free to say a hasty "No," so we flew to that city to meet with their board.

When we arrived, we found an alive group of people with big bold plans for the future, but they were meeting in a depressingly deteriorated building in a terribly unclean city with a drab and unappealing climate. We desperately wanted to do the will of God; however, we did not find it in our hearts to be excited about ministering in such a place.

We were sitting in the motel one morning when Elaine saw me pick up my Bible to have my devotions. Knowing how God speaks to me through His Word, she blurted out, "Oh, honey, find something that says, 'Go back'!"

I laughed, with mixed emotions struggling within me, and said, "Sweetheart, we don't look for what we *want* Him to say!"

"Oh, I know that!" she said.

Of course she did! She was as committed to the will of God as I was. She was just being honest with me about her feelings and expressing my own unexpressed ones, as well!

I opened my Bible to where the bookmark was, and to my amazement, the very first verse for that morning's reading was, "David then asked the Lord, 'Shall I *move back* to Judah?' And the Lord replied, 'Yes' " (2 Samuel 2:1, TLB). We felt immediately that the Lord was releasing us from this possibility of service. In the days that followed, further confirmations came to re-affirm that feeling.

Never make a decision that is based upon a verse of Scripture alone. You may have simply "chanced" upon it. On the other hand, never ignore verses that seem to apply to your situation, even when the words that have impressed you are being lifted out of their context. God's Word in combination with other confirmations can make a very solid foundation for decision-making.

Transition

1977

I will omit here some of the marvelous workings of God as He led us away from Anoka, Minnesota and up to Vancouver, British Columbia, Canada, since they are recorded in my earlier book entitled *How to Know God's Will*.

It was in the fall of 1977 that Elaine and I left the gorgeous five-bedroom parsonage on the lake there in Anoka, Minnesota and the wonderful people we had served at the Meadow Creek Church. Along with our son Gary we made the long drive across the country to the Pacific Northwest and then on up to our new home in Richmond, British Columbia where we would serve the Tenth Avenue Alliance Church in the city of Vancouver.

Our son Brian was at Moody Bible Institute where, in addition to his studies, he was courting a young lady from Chattanooga, Tennessee, who was lovely in every way. We could tell they were getting serious about each other, and we were quite happy about that. We found it so easy to both accept and love Connie.

How could we ever have dreamed that our ministry in this new country would be very brief, and that it was only further preparation for a specific, and at that time, most unusual ministry God had in mind for us in the very near future?

The God of All Comfort

1979

*F*orty years after the difficult experiences of surgery, body cast and confinement for the summer, God revealed *very clearly* what He had been doing those many years earlier! He did it through a phoned-in request. The phone message: "There is a Canadian Bible College student at the Royal Columbian Hospital in New Westminster. His name is Sean Campbell. He is home for the summer and was working under a car when the jacks failed and the car came crashing down, pinning him beneath it. He is in a body cast now from his neck all the way down to his hips. Would you mind stopping by to minister to him?"

Of course I wouldn't mind! I wasn't fully prepared, however, for the feelings that came over me when I stood by his bedside. The empathy I felt for that young man was deep and easily communicated to him. I had been where he was; I really knew what it was like. I recognized deeply for the first time that one of the reasons God had not healed me outright, but had allowed me to go through that summer, was that I might minister to Sean and many others with a greater depth of feeling. This truth became very real: " . . . the God of all comfort . . . comforts us in all our troubles, so that we can comfort those in any trouble with the comfort we ourselves have received from God" (2 Corinthians 1:3-4).

Transition

1979

I will omit here some of the marvelous workings of God as He led us away from Vancouver and down to Elizabethton, Tennessee, since they are recorded in my book *How to Know God's Will*.

It was in the fall of 1979 that Elaine and I sold almost all our belongings and moved 3,000 miles to start all over again. We were obeying God's explicit commands to our hearts. In some ways it was a frightening venture. In others it was a marvelous adventure, a growing experience.

The next few years were divided between establishing Fairhaven in Tennessee and going out for meetings whenever and wherever I was invited, so that this new ministry could become known around the country. I was often away from Elaine for one to three weeks at a time. She was sweet about it, though she didn't like those separations any more than I did. They were difficult years in some ways, but also ones beautifully filled with the blessings of the Lord.

1980-1994

Even when walking through the dark valley of death I will not be afraid, for you are close beside me, guarding, guiding all the way.
(Psalm 23:4, TLB)

A Heartwarming Experience

1980

A series of meetings in Hamlet, Nebraska was to be followed by a men's retreat at Glen Eyrie, the Navigators' fabulous castle in Colorado Springs. Two days and one night between those two speaking engagements would be mine to do with as I pleased.

A cheerful idea came to mind. I would rent a car and head for Estes Park, Colorado. There I would find a cabin with a fireplace and hibernate for twenty-four hours to prepare myself spiritually before going on to Glen Eyrie and my commitment there. Pastor and Mrs. Dennis Gordon insisted that I use their new car instead of renting one. He would get it back at the men's retreat. How very nice of them! For weeks beforehand I relished the thought of that time alone in the mountains beside a cozy fire.

The meetings were completed in Hamlet on a Wednesday night. Thursday morning I was ready to set out for Estes Park, but the weatherman said that a storm was moving into northern Colorado. I quickly changed my plans. I would go south toward Colorado Springs instead of heading in the direction of Estes Park. Perhaps I could avoid the storm that way.

Arriving in Colorado Springs, I checked with the Chamber of Commerce as to where there might be a

154

cottage with a fireplace. They named two places in Manitou Springs, a suburb. I checked them out and found that one was closed for the season. The other looked rather shabby. I drove on up into the mountains to Woodland Park and tried to find something there.

My precious hours were slipping away from me as I searched, and I was coming up with nothing suitable. *Lord Jesus, You know how much I would like to have a cottage with a fireplace. I don't understand why I am having such trouble. Please help me,* I prayed, expecting an answer to my prayer. He did not answer me, it seemed.

Snow began to swirl lazily in front of my headlights. I decided it would be better to go back down the mountain, and not chance getting stuck up there and risk missing my speaking engagement at Glen Eyrie. I felt a keen disappointment as I drove the winding road back down the mountain. I did try to remember that God can be in our disappointments as well as in our joys, but it is not easy to be completely victorious when you are so deeply disappointed. In fact, the deeper the disappointment the more God-given grace is needed to be thoroughly victorious.

Going through Manitou Springs on my way up the mountain, I had looked carefully at the exterior of the various motels. The nicest among them had been The Villa. I didn't even consider stopping there, since I was sure it would be too expensive. I always tried to use Fairhaven's funds carefully. When I came near The Villa, however, I felt a sudden urge to turn in and check their prices. I didn't think of that urge as a divine prompting. It was simply a recalling of the fact that sometimes, though not often, the nice places are not much more costly than the shabbier ones. At least there was no harm in checking.

A pleasant young fellow named Mark was at the desk. The price? $20 a night!

"May I see a room?" I asked, trying not to make too evident my pleasure over the very reasonable price he had quoted.

The room was really nice.

"I'll take it!" I said with the definiteness that comes from being decidedly pleased.

"For one night?" Mark asked.

"Yes," I said, "tomorrow I am going over to Glen Eyrie to speak to a group of men there."

"What will you be speaking about?" he asked.

"Well," I said, "it's a group of church men, and I'll be speaking to them from the Bible."

Mark's face lit up as he said, "I'm a Christian brethren, too!"

I wasn't certain whether that was a denomination or a person, but I assumed he meant a person. "Tell me about it, Mark. How did you become a Christian brethren?" I asked.

His answer thrilled me. "It happened shortly after my brother was killed by a car. In my shock and hurt, I felt desperately that I had to find meaning and truth somehow, so I began a diligent search. But no matter how hard I tried, I could not seem to find truth or meaning.

"On my way to class at college one day, I said to myself, *I cannot find meaning and truth by myself. I have exhausted all my resources. If they are to be found, somehow they are going to have to come to me.*

"When I arrived at class, a motivational tape was being played. The speaker was interesting and I enjoyed the things he had to say. At the very end of his talk, he made one statement that startled me. He suggested that we should read our Bibles every day. Immediately there was a strong response within me. *Perhaps that's it!* I thought. *Maybe the meaning of life and genuine truth are to be found in the Bible.*

"There had been a Bible at the head of my bed for a long time, but I had never read it. I picked it up with intense excitement. I turned to the first page and read, 'Pope Leo XIII granted to the faithful who shall read for at least a quarter of an hour the books of the Sacred Scripture with the veneration due to the Divine Word, and as spiritual reading, an indulgence of 300 days.' "

He was quoting from memory. I startled him by joining right in with him, *word for word!*

"Oh, are you a Catholic?" he asked.

I could have answered, "No, but I *am* a Christian brethren." Instead I said, "No, Mark, but our earthly affiliation is not what is important. It is our relationship to the living Christ that makes the difference." I could both sense and see his agreement with me.

"I didn't know the meaning of the word 'indulgence'," he continued, "but it seemed like a warm word. I turned to the next page where it said something about the Holy Spirit providing illumination to the sincere reader and suddenly I felt overwhelmed. With great excitement I realized that I had found meaning. *I had found the source of truth!*

"The room glowed with a light, and filled with a wonderful presence. In that moment I was reborn. The Holy

Spirit did indeed come to instruct me and to interpret to me. He showed me that these two sections, the Old Testament and the New Testament, were first prophecy and then prophecy fulfilled. He showed me the importance of studying the Scriptures."

I am slow to accept testimonies about bright lights and visionary experiences. But my heart was thrilled with the vibrance and vitality of this new Christian's understanding of the truth as he continued sharing with me, sprinkling his comments liberally with familiar scriptures that had become a part of him through diligent study. I felt a witness in my own spirit that this was very genuine.

He even told me that one of "our" maids—his parents owned The Villa—had noticed the change in his life and had asked him about it. When he told her he had become a "Christian brethren" she was delighted and said immediately, "Oh! Then you must ask God for the gift of tongues!" He told me he didn't know what she was talking about. She was insisting that a sincere Christian must ask God for this particular exotic gift.

He said, "I went back to my room and knelt and asked God if she was right. Once again my room filled with a bright light and a voice spoke to me and said, 'Turn to First Corinthians, chapter 12.' I didn't know where First Corinthians was in the Bible so I opened to the contents page and began to look. 'Genesis, Exodus, Leviticus . . .' I had to go a long way before I found First Corinthians, but when I did and opened to the twelfth chapter, my heart was so blessed, for it read, 'Now, concerning spiritual gifts, brothers, I do not want you to be ignorant.' The chapter was as clear as it could be, and before it ended it said so specifically which gifts are the greater ones. Then it read, 'eagerly desire the greater gifts.' I knew our maid was wrong. God had made it so clear."

"Mark," I enquired, "what time do you finish here at the front desk?"

"At 10 o'clock," he said.

"How about coming up to my room so we can have devotions together?"

"What do you mean by 'devotions'?" he asked.

I explained that we would read some from the Bible, discuss it together and then have prayer.

"I would like that!" he said.

We spent nearly an hour together in beautiful fellowship and meaningful prayer that night. I will never forget it. It was a heartwarming experience for both of us.

What had happened to my plans for a cottage with a fireplace? By direct intervention God had replaced them with something that warmed my heart instead of my toes. I had been privileged to strengthen Mark Dolan's hand in the Lord. Two "Christian brethren" had shared and prayed together.

I went on my way to Glen Eyrie that next morning rejoicing. When I shared this experience with the district-wide gathering of Alliance Men who had assembled there, an Air Force colonel, stationed at the Air Force base in Colorado Springs, asked me if he might disciple Mark. I was elated to see how God Himself had provided a very special follow-up for the meeting He had arranged the night before. God does all things well, and He does them thoroughly!

Special Delivery Mail

1980-83

We were on our way to Erie, Pennsylvania to have meetings there in the Alliance church where my good friend Bob Turner was pastoring. "Let's take two days to get there," I said to Elaine, "going as far as Pittsburgh the first day (an eight-hour drive) and then having lots of time the next day to stop and shop along the way."

She liked the idea.

I got out my Motel 6 book to see if they had a motel on the north side of Pittsburgh. They did! We decided we would try to stay there for the night. When we found it, to our relief there was a "Vacancy" sign lighted. But there was a small problem. Turns across the highway to the motel were not permitted. In fact they were not even possible, for there was a fence rising up out of the divider! We traveled almost a mile before we found a place to make a U-turn and head back to the motel. When we arrived there, the "Vacancy" sign had been turned off and a "No Vacancy" sign was lighted.

We were *so* disappointed! We headed on north, but found nothing. Each exit we came to was a point of hope until we got to it and found there just weren't any motels along that route. Finally I suggested that we get off the interstate and drive a few miles toward New Castle. Perhaps there would be something there. Again there was nothing!

We drove almost to New Castle itself, way beyond where we had planned to go. I was about to make another U-turn to head back to the interstate when we spotted an older motel. In desperation we stopped to check it out. It was clean and comfortable, and they even had candy and a local newspaper by the bed, and the price was right! We enjoyed it very much.

The next day we went on our way, praising the Lord for guiding our footsteps. Little did we know how very specifically He had guided those footsteps to a motel so far off our interstate route to Erie. No special outcome of staying in that particular motel was evident. That comes later, much later, perhaps a couple of years!

Now, let me tell you a completely different story. Later we will pull these stories together.

I was ministering at a conference in Pennsylvania. A pastor came to see me in private. "I am so deeply concerned for a colleague of mine whom I highly respect," he said. "He has a wonderful wife and family, but he has become involved emotionally with a neighbor girl who is only eighteen years old! Only he and his wife and the girl are aware of what is happening. That is, until recently. His wife could no longer keep her agony to herself and she told her mother. Her mother attends my church, and she has come to share it with me, swearing me to the strictest of confidence. I cannot even tell you who this pastor friend is."

I urged him to do his best to get permission for me to contact the pastor. "Please assure the mother, so she can assure her daughter, so she can assure her husband that I am a safe person for him to talk to. That's what Fairhaven is all about; we provide a safe place for persons to confess anything at all, without fear of retaliation or loss of job or other impact. I can be counted upon to keep his problem in strictest confidence. I want to help him through this crisis in his life."

The pastor assured me he would try to get permission to let me know who the man was so I could contact him and help him, but he felt fairly certain that it could not be arranged.

Now, let's hear a third story! Each March Elaine and I traveled to western Canada from Tennessee to participate in three banquets in Vancouver, Edmonton and Calgary. Some years special airfares for crossing Canada made it advantageous to drive to Toronto, leave our car at the airport and fly Air Canada from one coast to the other. The savings were substantial.

In 1983 that was the case. My friend Doug Miller pastored a large church in Morgantown, West Virginia. He had indicated an interest in our stopping there for a service sometime. So I wrote a letter to him to ask if the Sunday evening when we would be en route to Toronto would fit into his program. In case it would not, I also wrote a letter to that old motel near New Castle, asking (1) if it was still operated by the same couple, (2) if they still put candy by the bedside, (3) if they still had that nice tradition of providing a newspaper for their guests and (4) if the price was still the same, or had it gone up in the intervening years. Oh, and one more question: Would they have room for us on that particular Sunday night, if we were to travel that far instead of staying overnight in Morgantown? This was to be my backup in case Doug already had something planned for that night at his church and we could not have a service there.

Now is the time to reveal the significance of the title of this chapter—Special Delivery Mail. I picked up our mail, and to my amazement found in that one day's mail three very significant and definitely related letters. First, there was a letter from Doug Miller saying that he was so sorry, but since they were having their annual meeting of the church that night, it would not be the right time for us to come, obviously. Second, there was a letter from the owner of the motel on the outskirts of New Castle saying that they did indeed still own the motel and that we would find candy and a newspaper, and the same rate if we were to stop with them. Yes, they did have room for us that night and would be glad to have us stay there again. The third letter came from the troubled pastor whose friend had become involved with the eighteen-year-old neighbor girl. He said things were getting much worse and there was great danger of the home breaking up. In desperation the wife had given him permission for me to contact her husband. He revealed the name and location of the pastor to me. The location: *New Castle, Pennsylvania!* How could anyone be so blind as to fail to see that God had arranged it all?

I sent a letter to the troubled pastor and said that I felt it was God Himself who had done this amazing thing, because He loved him and wanted to help him. I told him the date that we would be arriving there and that I would plan to meet with him that night after getting settled in our motel. Over a three-year period

God had put all of this together so marvelously. *What a great God we have!*

I wish I could give you a happy ending to this, telling you that the marriage was saved because of all of this marvelous intervention on God's part. Unfortunately, I cannot. Even when God goes the extra mile to help His children, they must cooperate with His plan, or it is ineffective. God revealed to that pastor how very deeply He cared about him. However, the pastor was so thoroughly deceived by Satan that he refused God's help, and mine.

We stayed overnight in New Castle, not far from where that troubled man lived. Yet with help so near, he chose to reject it. That's tragic! I am amazed, though, at the love of God displayed in the intricate planning to help one of His sons who He knew would not even accept that help! It may be that the marvel of it all will get through to him yet. He knows all these details that I have related here.

1982

*F*rom its beginning, Fairhaven was a miracle of God. There were no appeals made for funds in the USA. Fairhaven of Canada, in a very low-key manner, would put out pledge cards at their banquets, but in the USA not even that was done. All bills were paid as God answered prayer and sent in the funds.

One day Elaine said to me, "Unless God sends us a large gift this month, we are going to default on our bills for the first time in Fairhaven's history." She kept the books. She knew!

I responded, "That will never happen. God will surely provide." I went over to the typewriter immediately and typed out the following note after dating it:

"To Whomever You Are:

"At this point I don't know who you are, but I know that out there somewhere is a faithful, sensitive Christian upon whom the Lord is going to place His hand, urging that person to give a sizable gift to this work so that our bills can be met this month.

"I want to thank you in advance for what you are going to do. May God richly bless you for it."

I laid the letter aside, and we continued our office work. A couple of weeks later, prior to the end of the month and in good time to take care of our outstanding bills, a sizable check arrived from Mr. George Dissette of Fort Myers, Florida. I got out the letter I had written and put a postscript on it as follows: "P.S. Nice to know who you are. Thanks for obeying the Lord!"

The next time I saw Mr. Dissette, with tears in his eyes he said, "Oh, suppose I had not obeyed God!"

I responded, "If you had not, you would have missed a great blessing and someone else would have received it in your place. God would not have failed us!"

Well, Well!

1982

*K*en Stumbo was the head of construction at Fairhaven. He and his wife, Gloria, were without question among the greatest blessings God ever gave to that ministry! Ken did a lot of reading in the early days of building the new campus, for he had never constructed a whole chalet before. Often he resorted to library books for the knowledge he needed.

When we had our first well drilled, we were thrilled to strike a good supply of water at only eighty feet. The well driller asked me if I wanted him to put in a submersible pump. "It would only cost $500 for a turn-key operation," he promised.

Ken was standing behind the man, and he vigorously shook his head, so I said "No, thanks. We will do that ourselves."

Afterward Ken said to me, "I don't know what's the matter with me. I must be out of my mind. I don't know how to do that!" Once again he went to the library to read up in preparation for a scary, unfamiliar project.

On Sunday evening, Ken was sitting next to one of our guests at the vesper service. After the service, as we were having refreshments, he remarked to the man, "I would appreciate your praying for me tomorrow. I have to put a pump at the bottom of our new well, and since I have never done anything like that before, I am nervous about it."

The man replied, "Do you have to do that project tomorrow?" The question was unusual.

Ken thought a moment, and said, "Well, not really. Why?"

"Because we are planning to spend tomorrow at Gatlinburg, and since I am in the well-drilling business, I'd be glad to help you, if you can wait until Tuesday," the man said.

We were thrilled, and, of course, Ken waited!

Nothing Shall Be Impossible

1982

I wanted the adjacent thirty-two acres so badly! Fairhaven's sixty-eight acres were gorgeous and were almost completely surrounded by United States Forestry land, so we had it made, except for those thirty-two downstream. If someone else were to purchase them we would have no control over what they would do with them. I earnestly asked the Lord to give them to us.

Richard Weicht, one of our board members, who realized the importance of our getting that acreage, said to me one day, "Make an offer up to $30,000 on that land. Linda and I will buy it personally and hold it for the day when Fairhaven wants to purchase it from us for the same amount that we paid for it."

I was thrilled, until I went to the realtor and made the offer! The owner, Betty Evans, was not impressed with my $22,500 offer. I increased the offer more than once, but she wanted $40,000, and not a penny less. Even when I reached our ultimate price of $30,000, she was totally unmoved from her position.

I asked our realtor if I might go talk to her personally.

"We do not like our clients to do that," he said, "but I am not getting anywhere with her at all, so why not?"

Betty lived in Oak Ridge, Tennessee. I called her mother in Elizabethton, where I lived, and learned that Betty would be coming for a visit the next week. I made an appointment to see her at her mother's home.

The visit took a strange twist. Very quickly Betty confided in me that she was suffering rather deeply from depression. I spent an hour or more dealing with that and urging her to come to Fairhaven so we could determine the level of care she should receive.

At that point she told me she was seeing a psychiatrist. She also told me there were a couple of men coming to her home each week for Bible studies.

I was immediately concerned. "Are they Jehovah's Witnesses, Betty?"

"No," she said, "that doesn't ring any bell."

"Would they be Mormons?"

"Yes! That's it! They call themselves 'Mormons.' "

I told her that their beliefs were not like the ones she learned as a child. I warned her of the dangers, and then asked if she would be willing to substitute a Bible class of my choosing that would be in keeping with the evangelical truths she had heard in her childhood.

She said she would.

I promised to write to her with a recommendation as quickly as I could find out what was available in Oak Ridge. Before leaving that day I said, "Betty, I came here to talk to you about the property you own adjacent to ours, up in the town of Roan Mountain. We really are interested in purchasing that, you know."

"Yes, I realize that," she said, "but I bought it for speculation and I am not willing to take a penny less than $40,000 for it."

I told her that if she should ever change her mind we would appreciate being the first to know of it.

She promised that we would.

I lost no time finding a Bible study for her. I wrote to a pastor in Oak Ridge explaining the need. He responded promptly with an address for me to give to her where a Bible study was being conducted that would be right for her. But his answer came one day too late! The night before, Betty had committed suicide!

I went over to try to comfort Mrs. Street, Betty's mother. I made no mention of the property we wanted or of our interest in it, of course. It was not an appropriate time.

A few months later I went back again, both to be a comfort and also to mention the property. "Mrs. Street, you know when Betty and I talked that day, the reason for my coming was to discuss the thirty-two acres she owned adjacent to ours in Roan Mountain."

"Yes, I know that," she responded. "Betty was not willing to sell that. She left it to me, however, and I am very willing to sell. What price were you discussing?"

"I had offered her $30,000," I replied.

"That will be fine!" she said immediately. "Just have your lawyers draw up the papers and I will sign."

What had seemed so impossible suddenly became a reality! And that was not the end of the story. A few years later Richard and Linda Weicht phoned me one day and instructed me to have the lawyers draw up new papers in Fairhaven's name. They were very generously donating that land to Fairhaven!

"Nothing shall be impossible!"

A Brush with the IRS

1982

*F*airhaven had been in operation for two-and-a-half years before my speaking engagement at a Missionary Church Association camp in Weeping Water, Nebraska. The man who provided the special music that week drove me to the Omaha airport after the meetings. It was on his own way home. En route he talked about his having incorporated as a nonprofit organization, as we had done. He asked me how I liked preparing the 990.

"What is the 990?" I asked.

He was horrified that I didn't know! He explained to me in graphic detail that it was a government report far worse than personal income tax and that it could take many days to complete. "It is an income tax form, of sorts, for nonprofit organizations, only you don't usually have to pay anything," he explained.

I determined to look into it right away.

Almost immediately following that conversation there came from the IRS a letter stating that we had not filed a 990, and that there was a $10 per day fine for failure to file. They said that we were now six months overdue from the filing deadline.

Having to pay an $1,800 fine for not filing information that I didn't know was required made me ill. God's people were supporting this new work and now must I waste $1,800 of their sacrificial gifts because I had been unaware of the horrendous 990? *Oh, Lord Jesus,* I prayed, *please help me somehow. I know that "ignorance of the law is no excuse" and we are liable for that fine, but I feel terrible about having to use Your money this way simply because of my own ignorance. Please help me!*

Almost immediately there flashed into my mind a conversation with someone during which he had revealed that he was a fairly recent retiree from the IRS. It seemed to me that he had been a rather high-up official. But I could not remember who he was, or where he lived in our big country. It was when I was in meetings *somewhere* that I had met him, I felt, but where?

I continued to pray, and then suddenly I knew. It was John West from the Alliance Bible Fellowship in Boone, North Carolina, less than an hour's drive from Fairhaven! I picked up the phone immediately and called him. I explained to him my situation.

He responded, "Can you come over to have lunch with me tomorrow?"

"You bet!"

After a nice lunch together, John took me back to the church office, picked up the phone and called Washington. I heard him say, "Hello, Sarah, is the boss in?"

There was a pause.

"Well, Sarah, this is something you can take care of for me. There is this true-blue organization known as Fairhaven Ministries. The director was not aware of the need of filing a 990. It was an honest omission. This is not the type of organization we go after. They are being fined $1,800 for not filing. Can you take care of that for me? Thanks, Sarah!"

He informed me that I would be receiving a phone call from the regional office the next morning.

It came, and a gracious lady said, "I understand you are facing a fine, but that you didn't even know you were to file the form. Please take down this letter that I dictate to you, word for word and mail it to me today."

It was a letter to herself from me. It included specialized terms that were totally new to me. It stated beautifully what had happened and requested that the fine be waived—no, that was not the word; it was a term I had never heard, but that's what it meant.

I mailed it to her promptly.

Her answer—to her own letter—came back just as promptly. In His own marvelous way, God turned a terrible error on my part into a gracious forgiveness on the IRS's part.

I am fully convinced that there is nothing too difficult for the Lord.

Above What You Ask or Think

1983

Elaine's statement was dramatic: "Unless we receive $435 today we will not be able to pay the Fairhaven bills that are due now!" She was doing the bookkeeping and was concerned.

"Well, let's see what's here in the mail," I suggested. There were five pieces of mail. The first one I laid aside. The return address told me all I needed to know. That faithful Fairhaven backer sent a $100 check each month as regularly as clockwork.

"Now we only need $335," I remarked.

I opened the next envelope and found a request for information about Fairhaven. The third item was a cleverly disguised bit of junk mail. Envelope number four contained a warm note of thanks from two persons who had come to our retreat center for help.

There was only one piece of mail left to open. I slit the top of it with great expectation, but there was no check in it. "Well," I said, "God will have to work in some other way to provide for our needs today."

Then I opened that first piece of mail which I had felt so sure would have $100 in it. To my amazement I found a check in the amount of $535. It was the $435 we needed to pay our bills, plus the usual $100. God had once again done "exceeding abundantly above all that we ask or think" (Ephesians 3:20, KJV).

A "Private Chaplain"

1983

*T*he land we had purchased on which to build the Fairhaven village was up above Moody Aviation on Holston Mountain. There were some magnificent views of the airstrip and of distant mountains. The terrain was somewhat steep, but it could be developed beautifully. There was a major hurdle to that development, however. When Fairhaven grew to the point where we needed to start construction, we discovered that we did not have legal access to the property!

I went up into Minton Hollow one day to hike on our land and found that our entrance was gone. The whole area where we had been told we had access to the property had been turned into an expansion of a neighbor's lawn. I was really upset!

I went to the neighbor's house and was told that he had paid to have it surveyed, and this was indeed his land and not ours.

Further checking confirmed that he was right. We had no legal access! It was a most distressing turn of events. We had used contributions from the Lord's people. Some had been sacrificially given. We had paid $28,500 to make that purchase, and now it was valueless to us for building purposes.

We bought another, much more beautiful piece of property with a stream running through it that was appropriately named "Roaring Creek." Though I enjoyed the new property and the developing of it, there continually ran through my mind the gnawing thoughts: *Why did I purchase that property on Holston Mountain? How could I have felt so certain that it was the Lord's will for us? How could I have been so wrong? What a waste of money!*

Actually the "wrong" was in my current thinking. As always, God knew exactly what He was doing, even when I did not.

One day the phone rang. There was a young man on the other end of the line. "Are you the owner of the fifty acres up on Holston Mountain above Moody Aviation?" he asked.

"Yes," I responded.

"Well, I would like to take a look at that when you have time. Would you have time to walk it with me this noon on my lunch hour?"

You can be sure that I *made* the time to do it! I was *very* eager to sell that property, and was excited that someone was interested.

Marv and I hiked all over the steep acreage that noon. We became quite tired and sat down on a large rock to talk. I later learned that rattlesnakes had a den beneath that rock and it was called "Rattlesnake Rock," as they liked to come out and sun themselves there!

Our conversation turned to spiritual matters. We had a most enjoyable talk. That was the first of many. Marv never did purchase that land. As of this writing we still own it, a dozen years later.

He found another beautiful site on which to build a lovely home. But Marv and I kept up our friendship. Always our conversation centered around the Lord. He began to call me his "private chaplain", based on a verse he discovered in The Living Bible that speaks of Nathan's relationship to David. Nathan was called David's "private chaplain."

Marv has grown in the Lord through the years and it has been a great joy to know him. I am convinced that God led me to purchase the property so that we could meet and enjoy this spiritually profitable relationship.

But that's not all! One day Marv called me and asked, "Do you have a few minutes? May I drop by your house?"

"Sure!" I said.

He didn't stay long. He just wanted to hand me an envelope. As he gave it to me, he said, "I really believe in what you are doing!"

Then he said, "Open it."

I did. It was full of money!

"Count it!" he ordered, with a smile. There was $2,500 in that envelope. I was overwhelmed!

A few weeks later Marv did that again.

Over the years, to the time of the writing of this chapter, Marv has given to Fairhaven more than $100,000! God knew what He was doing when He placed a strong impression upon my heart that Fairhaven should purchase those fifty acres. That initial investment of $28,500 has produced spiritual returns that are far more valuable even than the monetary ones.

"As for God, His ways are perfect!" the Bible says. I can say a hearty "amen" to that.

Cash and Carry Only!

1983

The Meadow Creek Chalet was all furnished except for the loft. We had even used the main floor a few times. Now, however, we could not delay even one more day the purchasing of the twin beds for the loft. Dr. McCarthy, the Academic Dean of Toccoa Falls College, along with his wife and their daughter, a nurse, were arriving at Fairhaven. We had assigned them to this, our first chalet, and needed both floors.

"We have only $16 in our checking account, and those beds will cost us $366," I reminded Elaine. We prayed together that God would provide the $350 we were short. Very graciously the owner of the company that produced the excellent quality bedding we were to purchase had agreed to sell to us wholesale, but it was strictly "cash and carry." We had to make full payment for the beds when we picked them up at the local factory.

The mail came. In it was an envelope from a lady who so faithfully sent her monthly contribution of $5. We always appreciated her sacrificial giving. Imagine my surprise upon opening her letter to find in it a check for $350! There was no explanation. The next month she was back to her regular $5. But when we had that urgent need, God entrusted her with extra money and she did with it what He asked her to do!

Oh, No! A Drunk!

1984

We were not really too unhappy about the inability of our travel agent to find us a midmorning flight back from the West Coast. It could actually be fun to rent a very reasonable subcompact car and spend the day exploring the Los Angeles area.

So much for the delightful fantasy! We were brought back to harsh reality quickly when we tried to rent a car. All the major car rental companies had the same story: "No cars available."

Undaunted, I started phoning the smaller rental agencies that had their car lots away from the airport. The story was the same everywhere: "No cars available." Never before nor since have I encountered a time when there was not a car to be found in the whole city.

We went to the airline counter and asked if there was any possibility of an earlier flight. Were they booked solidly? Could we be listed as standbys? The answer was not at all encouraging. All flights were filled to capacity. Some were even overbooked, we were informed. They advised us simply to forget about getting anything earlier than that evening "red-eye" flight.

"When does the next flight leave?" I asked.

"At 12:30, but it is very full. Your chances would be slim."

I asked him if he could check us in for the evening flight, so we could get rid of our baggage, and then wait-list us for that midday one.

He agreed, but reluctantly.

We went up to the gate area and turned our names in there, too, for standby status. Shortly after 12 they boarded the plane. We waited and waited, and at the last minute, the agent called our names. *Three cheers!* We boarded, so pleased to have seats.

To our amazement, things were not as bad as we had been told. We had a window and center seat. The seat beside me was empty. On up the aisle toward the front there were two more empty aisle seats.

They had actually closed the doors, and I was just about to move over to the aisle so Elaine and I could have lots of elbow room when they reopened the door to receive one last passenger. It was a young man, approximately college age, I guessed. He came down the aisle, bypassing both of those empty seats and plopped down in the seat beside me. He reeked of alcohol. "Oh, no! A drunk!" I whispered in Elaine's ear.

That fairly drunk young man was talkative, as most drunks are. He told me he was going home to Pennsylvania for one last visit with his dying mom. He breathed alcohol fumes in my face as he spoke. It was really obnoxious.

"She's really religious, you know!" he told me. "But I don't believe the way she does anymore. I've gotten interested in some of these eastern religions we have out here in California. I don't go home anymore because she wants to talk to me about it, and I don't want to hear it. It upsets her that I drink, too."

"Where in Pennsylvania is your home?" I asked.

"State College," he replied.

"I visited State College about a year ago," I told him. "What church does your mother go to?"

"The Alliance church," he said. That was the very church where I had preached a series of messages the year before! Suddenly the pieces of the puzzle fit together: why there had been no rental cars available and why this boy had passed up the other two empty aisle seats. He was easy to witness to, for in his semi-inebriated condition, he was very talkative. God wonderfully helped me in the witnessing.

After we got home, I immediately contacted the youth pastor at that church, knowing the boy was going to be home for a week. I asked him to follow up my witness. He did, faithfully, and in the hospital room by his dying mother's bedside, that young man came back to the Lord.

I wish I had been more spiritual in my response to that last minute appearance of the young man on the plane. My response should not have been, "Oh, no! A drunk!" It should have been, "Thank God! A drunk!"

"Man looks at the outward appearance, but the LORD looks at the heart" (1 Samuel 16:7). This boy's heart was badly in need of cleansing. God wanted me to have a part in the softening of his heart in preparation for a new work He planned to do. Unfortunately I was not in tune with God's plans. Thankfully, in His mercy, God chose to use me in spite of my attitude!

"Heather" and "Mary"

1985

The most traumatic counseling situations I encountered while ministering to ministers and their wives at Fairhaven were the devastations of extramarital affairs. One pastor's wife was especially shattered. Her husband was perhaps the most highly respected pastor in the district where they served. She had not the slightest clue of his multiple involvements with women in their last three pastorates. When it all came to light, she was practically destroyed. He was terribly chagrined and embarrassed over his sexual addiction and appeared to be genuinely repentant.

At one point I asked her, "Do you have some woman in whom you can confide when you get back home, who will be a support person for you?"

To my surprise, my questioned triggered sobbing. "No," she blurted out, "every one of my best friends are women with whom he became intimately involved!"

"You must have someone to talk to," I insisted. "Would you give me permission to write to a pastor's wife who was here six months ago in almost an identical situation to yours? Her husband was also involved with a half dozen women in more than one of their pastorates. She has been through what you are going through and God has helped her and her husband wonderfully. It may be that she will feel sufficiently healed that she

183

would be willing to talk with you, or correspond with you. I will refer to her as 'Mary' and for now when I talk with her, I will call you 'Heather.' "

"I'd like that," was her unhesitating response.

So I wrote to "Mary" and told her about "Heather," but I didn't press her into this ministry of helping. I was well aware that a person has to do some healing before she (or he) is ready to help someone else.

Mary wrote back, "I'd love to do that. It would help to put some meaning into what has happened in my life, if it could be used of the Lord to help someone else."

So, I sent "Heather's" real name and address to "Mary." I also wrote "Heather" and told her who "Mary" was, and that she was willing to correspond with her. They lived 2,000 miles apart. When the two ladies received my letters, they both sat down and wept. They knew each other! In fact, they knew each other *well*. They had attended the same Bible college together. They had sung in the same trio. They had traveled together for their college one summer. They were good friends!

I knew none of that, but God did! He was the one who had arranged this special comfort for them both. One had access to a WATTS line, so they very quickly were on the line together and spent the next three hours in conversation. They became a major source of strength and help to each other.

Jesus didn't stop caring about His "Marys" and "Heathers" when He returned to heaven. He knows what we have need of, and in our darkest hour comes to our relief in the most beautiful of ways.

A Double Blessing

1986

*T*here were four couples to be counseled that morning at Fairhaven and I knew the importance of my meeting God personally before heading out to the campus to try to help others. God impressed a verse upon my heart, as He does every morning. I meditated on it, and then wrote my one-page journal of thoughts about it. I decided to print an extra copy and take it along with me, just in case somewhere along the way it might be useful to one of the counselees.

One of the four couples that were scheduled I would be seeing for the first time. I had no advance information on what the problem was. After visiting with three couples, I completely forgot about the printout that lay on the front seat of my car. I went in to meet this new couple and was soon engrossed in what the husband was telling me. He talked about his lack of confidence in himself, his repeated depressions and the poor relationship he had with his father. He could never please his dad. Nothing was ever good enough for him.

I asked him if he had any idea how his grandfather treated his father.

"Strangely, I *do* know," he said, "my dad never talked deeply with me except on one occasion when he opened up and told me how his father had treated him. It was exactly as he was treating me!"

I asked if he knew how his great-grandfather had treated his grandfather.

He didn't know. That was too far removed.

"I have one more question for you," I said. "You have a twelve-year-old son. How do you treat him?"

He began to cry. "I find myself doing the same thing to him, and I hate it!" he grieved.

I told him that I have a theory that I call the "chain theory." I pointed out that there seems to be a chain formed generation by generation. Somewhere along the line that chain must be broken by a person who refuses to become *bitter* and who insists upon becoming *better* as a result of his childhood experiences. He must determine, "By the grace of God, I will not forge another link in this burdensome chain!"

The chain that binds generation after generation into the same pattern became our main topic of conversation for awhile. Then I remembered my devotional journal!

"Wait a minute!" I said with great excitement, "I have something for you!"

I went out to the front seat of my car and brought in the journal page I had written that morning. I was thrilled along with him as I read it aloud. It read:

> "Free yourself from the chains on your neck, O captive" (Isaiah 52:2).
>
> What a challenge! Father, it is so foolish for people who are Yours by Your choice (and then by theirs) to permit any bondage, when You have promised all the power needed to free themselves from that bondage.

Why should any habit control me? Why should depressions make life miserable? Why should a lack of confidence be a chain about my neck holding me back? There is no reason.

I notice that I missed an earlier challenge here, "O Zion, clothe yourself with strength." What a privilege to put on Your strength and then, clothed in that strength, to free myself from the chains.

It becomes a matter of claiming what is rightfully mine in the Lord, for it is already provided for me and offered to me. Oh, why do I so often live beneath my rights and privileges?

This day I will, by Your grace and with Your enabling, clothe myself with strength. I will shake off the chains that would hold me back from being a really free-spirited person, operating in the fullness of freedom provided for me through my Savior's completed work at Calvary!

We wept together to think that God would have given to me that very morning, before ever meeting this hurting Christian, a verse speaking so directly to the issues of lack of confidence, depressions and especially the "chains" that bind!

The Dogwood Chalet

1986

We had only $500. That was enough to rent a backhoe and dig the footings for the new Dogwood Chalet. It would also pay for the cement for those footings and buy some blocks for the foundation, so we began construction. The funds came in steadily for awhile. Then suddenly we had only $300 left.

"Don't order any more materials," I told Ken Stumbo, who headed up the construction.

He informed me that we already had enough materials on hand for two more weeks of work.

"Good!" I said. "That gives us two weeks to pray."

Ken responded, "The next things I need to order are the Andersen windows and they will cost about $2,300."

We were $2,000 short of that.

I headed for Minneapolis to speak at a conference for Bethany Fellowship. "Lord Jesus," I prayed, "would it please You to have them give me an honorarium of $1,000 this time instead of the usual $250 to $400? That would mean that we would have one-half of the remaining funds we need for those windows."

On the return plane trip, I opened the envelope containing the gracious thank-you and the honorarium check. It was for $2,000! I was reminded of His promise "to do immeasurably more than all we ask or imagine, according to his power . . . " (Ephesians 3:20). The Dogwood Chalet went on to completion and was dedicated debt-free. In fact, every building on the grounds that has been built through the years has been dedicated without indebtedness to the glory of the Lord.

1988

With only $5,000 in hand, we started to build the quarter-of-a-million dollar lodge at Fairhaven. Once again we had enough to bulldoze the hole, backhoe the footings, pour cement and buy some block. The flow of funds in answer to prayer kept Ken Stumbo and his construction workers in supplies for many months. However, we were still lacking about $30,000 to complete the lodge.

One day Steven Zub, a board member of Fairhaven of Canada, suggested that I ask Samaritan's Purse for some funds.

"There are two reasons for not doing that, Steve," I said. "We don't ask man for money, and I don't think Samaritan's Purse has projects in the homeland. I think it invests only overseas."

Steve felt I was wrong on both counts. He knew that they had some projects in the homeland, for one thing. For another, he felt preparing a proposal for an organization that was looking for worthy projects was not the same as asking individuals for money.

I didn't want to be stubborn about it, so I put it on my prayer list: "Samaritan's Purse—$10,000." I also put on my list of things to get done: "Prepare a proposal for Samaritan's Purse." I prayed daily, but I also procrastinated daily and never got around to making that proposal.

The Alliance Bible Fellowship in Boone, North Carolina telephoned to ask if I would preach on Sundays for them for the next few months whenever I was not out somewhere representing Fairhaven. Their pastor had moved away. They thought it might take six months to find their next one. They felt my coming as often as possible would provide some continuity.

I readily agreed to this arrangement. It was only an hour's drive from Fairhaven. Franklin Graham, the head of Samaritan's Purse, attended that fellowship! God coordinated our schedules so that I was the speaker whenever he was at home. When I was traveling, so was he, with only a couple of exceptions.

In each of the services I told just a little bit about what God was doing for and through Fairhaven. I reported on the progress we were making on the lodge, but never once asked people to give toward it.

On Easter Sunday, following the service, Franklin came to me with tears in his eyes. "I think God would have us help you with the construction of that lodge," he said. "If you will stop by my office, we will have a check ready for you for $20,000."

A few months later the lodge at Fairhaven was dedicated debt-free, without our ever having had to ask for a single penny for its construction or for its furnishings. "[M]y God will meet all your needs according to his glorious riches in Christ Jesus" (Philippians 4:19). "Now to him who is able to do immeasurably more than all we ask or imagine, according to his power that is at work within us, to him be glory in the church and in Christ Jesus throughout all generations, for ever and ever! Amen" (Ephesians 3:20-21).

Never Too Late

1988

The closer it came to the end of the summer, the more concerned we became. We needed a new host and hostess for Fair-haven. I reassured Elaine that God would provide His own couple for this and would not fail us. That was easy for me to say, but it was difficult for her to believe. There were just too many things that had to come together. For example: our staff had to raise their own support. That in itself could take up to a year. But they needed to be on duty in three months.

The nearer it came to the deadline, the more difficult it was for *me* to believe, as well. How could God provide a couple now, when it was less than a month until we needed them? They could never get their support raised that fast! It looked like an impossibility. We kept on praying, but I am afraid our faith level went down, along with the number of days remaining.

Only two weeks before our deadline I began a series of tent meetings in Dalbo, Minnesota. I knew very few of the people who came, even though there were nearly 450 people attending nightly. I was so pleased one night as we approached the tent to see some former students of mine who were home on furlough from Brazil.

"Bob and Shirley!" I exclaimed. "It's so good to see you! You're returning to the field soon, aren't you? When do you leave?"

Shirley answered with emotion, "This morning!"

I couldn't understand, for it was now evening.

"I have the plane tickets right here in my pocketbook," Shirley continued, tears in her eyes.

I had to head for the platform, so I said, "We need to talk. Could we have lunch together tomorrow?"

They agreed.

The next day the four of us went out for lunch and they told Elaine and me a very sad story. They had come to the end of their furlough time, had arranged their flights back to Brazil, had sold their car and house furnishings, had closed up their apartment and prepared to leave. Then, unexpectedly, there had come a message from the headquarters of their mission stating that the medical doctor for the mission felt Bob should stay home another year to permit complete healing for his stomach ulcer. They were not to go back at this time!

"Why didn't they tell us before we sold our car and left our home? We don't know where we will live or what we will do for these twelve months!" Shirley said.

I looked over at Elaine and smiled. I told the Kallems about our need at Fairhaven for a host and hostess and asked if they would consider coming on our staff.

They were thrilled! Their mission would be paying their monthly salary during the enforced medical leave.

God had once again provided marvelously and just in the nick of time. He is *never* too late. Even when we begin to see something as "impossible," we have to remind ourselves that the word "impossible" doesn't even exist in God's vocabulary. That's a totally human concept.

Oh, God, I Need...

1988

*T*he day we were told by Dr. Haibach that the severe pain in my sweetheart's neck was cancer, not arthritis, was probably the darkest day of our lives. He said it had already metastasized to her skeletal frame in numerous places and was in a very advanced stage.

We sat in our car in front of the doctor's office in Boone, North Carolina and cried together. I drove to the drug store to get the rigid Philadelphia collar that would hold her head immobile during the sixty-mile ride to the Johnson City Cancer Center. I was instructed to go around curves carefully and to avoid bumps, as there was imminent danger of her neck breaking!

After I thought I had gained control of my emotions and before beginning the drive, I phoned to inform our staff at Fairhaven of our heartbreaking news and to ask for their prayers. When Gloria Stumbo answered, I tried to tell her, but I could not control my tears. She wept along with me.

The oncologist who met us in the emergency room frightened us with his honest, straightforward appraisal of how extremely serious the situation was. Elaine would have to be admitted to the hospital immediately for a series of tests—MRI, CAT scan, X rays, blood work, etc. If the cancer had already invaded the nerve linings to the brain, she could die within an hour, he said!

He would begin emergency radiation immediately, bringing in an off-duty technician. Chemotherapy would be necessary. I followed my honey's wheelchair down the long corridors to the admitting area, hardly able to comprehend that this nightmare was real.

I was standing behind her as she sat in that wheelchair answering the many questions they insist upon asking, no matter how sick you are. My heart was breaking over the prospect of losing the darling of my heart. The devastating prognosis of Dr. Haibach was still ringing in my ears: "You may have eight good months left together." Even worse than that was the frank statement by Dr. Ortega that Elaine might live less than an hour!

There was no one with us. One of our sons, Gary, lived in Minneapolis, 1,200 miles away. The other son, Brian, was an MAF pilot down in the jungles of Ecuador. Though he lived in Puyo, the capital of the region, there was no phone where I could reach him! I felt as though my bottled-up emotions were about to burst my chest! I cried out to God with an honest but totally unrealistic plea, "Oh God, I need a man on whose chest I can lay my head and cry!"

I turned my back to the whole scene before me to hide my tears from my honey and to blot out momentarily the visual evidence of our nightmare. As I did, the double doors behind us swung open and through them came Rick Erickson, a friend who lived 1,200 miles away. He had a big, beautiful pot of chrysanthemums cradled in

one arm. I laid my head against his chest and sobbed silently so my honey could not hear me.

When I think of the phenomenal logistics involved
in arranging for Rick to come through those doors as
soon as I had finished my own prayer of, "Oh God, I
need . . . ," I am amazed and humbled. Rick and Sandy
had just completed the grueling twenty-four-hour
drive from Minneapolis, nonstop, and had arrived at
Fairhaven, thirty-five miles from the hospital, very
weary. Gloria had received my call shortly before.
Upon hearing the news, Rick had gotten right back in
his van and, ignoring his own tiredness, had driven the
forty-five minutes to the Medical Center, bringing
with him that beautiful plant. In that large hospital
complex he had enquired as to our whereabouts and
finally had found us at precisely the right moment to
be the answer to my specific prayer, a split-second after it had been expressed! No wonder our God calls
Himself "the God of all comfort"(2 Corinthians 1:3).

Our Wonderful "Boss"

1988

*T*he months that followed the staggering diagnosis of cancer produced a whirlwind of painful memories. I don't like to talk about them to this day.

Elaine's neck was in danger of breaking at any moment, so they immediately began radiation treatments. When I say "immediately," I mean it! Though all technicians were off for the weekend, they summoned one back to Johnson City from his home in Bristol to start the radiation on Saturday!

As soon as the ten radiation treatments were completed and Elaine's horribly sore throat had healed, they inserted a portacath beneath the skin and started chemotherapy treatments for a year. I will spare you (and me) the details of the horrors of that. The powerful chemicals they injected into her veins caused almost all of her hair to come out. We bought a good quality wig well ahead of time in preparation for that humiliating facet of cancer treatment.

I remembered the words of Dr. Haibach the day he diagnosed the cancer: "You may have eight good months left together." Those words were so devastating to me that I would not even repeat them to anyone for months and months. I almost denied them to myself. I didn't tell Elaine, not to hide it from her, but because I was repressing them and denying them.

Six months later, Dr. Ortega, one of our oncologists, examined Elaine one day and then said, "This is little short of miraculous. I remember how bad you were the day you came in to Emergency. Your 'Boss' up there is really doing something!"

We were thrilled to hear this man, for whom swearing was a normal part of conversation, having to give God the glory for what He was doing.

Elaine lived more than twelve times longer than the doctor had originally said. Four years after that shattering diagnosis, she was doing remarkably well, with great improvement over the day when Dr. Ortega first saw her in the emergency room. Our wonderful " 'Boss' up there" was the reason. We want never to forget that we are His servants (and not just his employees, as Dr. Ortega's term might imply) and that He dealt with us most graciously in answer to our earnest prayers. The cancer eventually took my dear sweetheart's life, but the timing was not in keeping with the predictions of the doctors. God Himself is the One who decides how long we shall live, and even the worst diseases cannot change that!

The Children's Bread

1988

The verse that includes the words, "the children's bread," referring to divine healing, will forever bring goose bumps to my flesh when I come across it, because . . . well, let me just share my devotions from that day when I encountered these words during my twelve-year walk through the Bible. But first, I think a little more background would help you feel it as I felt it that day in 1988.

The diagnosis of cancer had left us with a shattered world. "Eight good months left together" were heartrending words to two people as deeply in love as my sweetheart and I were. I begged God to let us have one more Christmas together as a family. *Please let us travel to Ecuador to be with Brian and Connie and our grandchildren*, I implored. We would take our other son, Gary, down with us and the whole family would be together one more time.

I made a three-foot-tall thermometer-type chart with a space for every day until the day we would board the plane. We would live by faith, one day at a time. Each evening I colored in the day: *green* was for a good day, *yellow* was for a not-so-good one and *red* was for those terrible days after chemotherapy. The thermometer slowly but surely filled in—one-quarter full, half full, three-quarters full.

Finally the last day was colored in! My honey was not only still alive, but also she was able to travel, though weak and still on chemotherapy. Our oncologist had herself grown up on the mission field in India. She agreed to let Elaine have her chemotherapy there in Ecuador by pills this one time, instead of intravenously.

Now, instead of my telling you the marvelous story, let my devotional journal written on that day tell it like it was.

Devotional Journal for December 15, 1988 (Mark 7:26-27)

The woman was a Greek, born in Syrian Phoenicia. She begged Jesus to drive the demon out of her daughter. "First let the children eat all they want," he told her, "for it is not right to take *the children's bread* and toss it to their dogs."

Lord Jesus, I am thrilled that today in a very special way we are partaking of "the children's bread!" We are Your children, by Your grace, and because of Your divine choice, as well as by an act of our wills in receiving You. We are your children on the strength of Your words: "[T]o all who received him, to those who believed in his name, he gave the right to become children of God" (John 1:12).

We are "children of God," Elaine and I, and we have a right to "the children's bread."

I am nearly in tears as I write, tears of joy, for today we leave for South America in three and one-half hours, and it is only because You have heard our earnest prayers about it.

I know that my honey is doing so well because

You have willed it! I remember the words of our oncologist, "Little short of a miracle," and I rejoice to agree with him that, "Your *Boss* up there is really doing something!" *Oh, praise Your name!*

Last night Elaine slept soundly all night with just a half of a sleeping pill. She needed that only because she was so excited! A few months back, when she moaned all night, I lay on the floor beside her chair and gave her heavy, powerful painkillers every three hours. Now we are about to board that plane for a very happy Christmas! Precious Lord, how ever do I say a big enough "Thank You, Jesus, for all You've done"?

I think I hear Your answer: "Believe me for a marvelous New Year filled with healing, too!"

Yes, we're Your children. You've given us *the children's bread!*

Written later in the day . . .

We left from Tri Cities Airport today. I felt in my heart that it would be a great thrill if You would arrange to have a Boeing 727 take us. It would confirm Mark 7:27 to my heart in a very special way. It would be the icing on the cake!

We walked out to the plane. It was not a 727, but a Folker F28 that we boarded. *Oh, well,* I thought, *that would have been nice, but we're happy enough just to be going.* Then I realized that we had one more domestic flight after changing planes in Charlotte.

As we pulled up to the gate in Charlotte I looked out the window and saw a 727. It had the numbers painted on its tail, as well as the right configuration. Our flight to Miami, however, was to be on an entirely different concourse. When we got over there I could see the plane we would be getting on and it did not match the lines and shape of the 727 I had seen. I realized that we were not going to have that delicious "icing on the cake" that I had hoped for.

Strangely, I was wrong! Once we were settled in our seats, I pulled out the laminated card that described our plane. I knew immediately that I had to save that card for my "memories" file. The plane was a 727-200, or 727-B. What a thrill I felt in my soul!

The biblical mention of the "children's bread" is in the latter part of Mark 7:27. I know some people would chalk that up to coincidence, but I wonder what the statistical probability is of reading through the Bible and on the day you come to chapter 7 and verse 27 of *any* book, not only boarding a 727, but also having the text relate very specifically to the significance of the trip you are taking that day?

I know You did this for us, dear Lord, and I revel in Your personal way of caring, and the clever ways by which You let Your "gentle whisper" (or "still small voice") be heard.

1990

W hen life would get humdrum, or even hint at it, Elaine and I would just go someplace special. We had time-proven places that appealed to us. This time we chose The Innkeeper, a motel that sat between two places where we liked to shop, and right next to a wonderful K&W Cafeteria over in Winston-Salem, North Carolina. It was a motel that fit our budget wonderfully at $19 a night for two, so we decided we would go there for a two-night stay and just relax, watch TV, shop, play games and sleep in as long as we wished in the morning.

We drove the three and one-half hours, pulled in to The Innkeeper's parking lot, and to our dismay found they had raised their prices $10 per night! That did _not_ fit our economy budget. I dropped my sweetheart off to shop while I drove out to see if there might be a clean, comfortable, more reasonably priced motel on the outskirts of the city. I asked the Lord to guide me.

Very quickly the city was left behind. Now there were only fields on both sides of the road! I approached a country church, where there were cars pulling into the parking lot. I wondered why they were there in midafternoon. A wedding, perhaps? I decided to pull in and boldly ask some arriving people where I could find the kind of motel I was looking for. These would be local people. Perhaps they would know.

The next car that arrived held a man and his wife and a small child. I approached him and told him what I was looking for. He assured me there wasn't anything more reasonable than the $29 they were now asking at The Innkeeper. He said that way up on the north side of town there was a Holiday Inn that might be about the same price, but he doubted that it would be less.

He asked where I was from and what my work was. When I told him about our retreat center for pastors and missionaries, he showed a lot of interest. He confided that he had wanted to serve the Lord someday himself, but the door had not opened as yet. He was seeking the Lord's guidance for his future. I assured him I would remember him in prayer.

I thanked him for his help and as I turned to go back to my car, he said, "Just a minute! I want you to stay at The Innkeeper these two nights." He reached for his wallet and pulled out a $20 bill! "God gave me some extra money this week, and I feel He wants me to share it with you. This will cover the extra $10 per night."

When I picked up my honey, after checking in at The Innkeeper, I said, "You would never in a hundred years dream of what has happened. We are staying at The Innkeeper and it is costing us only $19 a night!"

God had used Steve Clayton, a complete stranger, to make our mini-vacation all the more enjoyable. When we returned to Elizabethton, I sent Steve my book, *How to Know God's Will*, along with my thanks.

I marvel at the timing of the Lord to bring us together in that church parking lot. Who can deny that our steps are "ordered by the LORD"(Psalm 37:23, KJV)?

Overweight Again

1991

Why is it that every time we go to a mission field our baggage is overweight, or at least dangerously close to it? I suppose when I think about it, the answer is obvious: We love to take things the missionaries cannot get on their field and to see the joy that something as simple as chocolate chips for baking, or a bottle of vanilla, can bring. Also there are people who learn that we are going and they ask if we can take a little something for their children. Sometimes that "little something" turns out to be pretty big!

When our grandchildren were small, we enjoyed the tradition we established by taking a daily gift for them, whenever we headed for Ecuador. That took space also. If there was any room left, we felt we really needed to take a few clothes to wear while we were down there!

It was on the trip to Ecuador in the fall of 1991 that I realized we were considerably overweight. In fact, we had five suitcases instead of the four we were allowed, and some of those weighed a "ton!" I knew we would be charged heavily for being overweight unless my friend would be the clerk we would get at the airport.

"Lord, please let Dave be the one to check us in," I prayed. I knew there was only about one chance in ten of that happening, humanly speaking, but God could arrange it. Somehow I believed He would.

When we arrived at the airport I lugged the five suit-cases in from the curb at the risk of a hernia. I saw nothing of Dave. Perhaps he was down in baggage instead of at the counter, or maybe it was even his day off.

The man who checked me in was very pleasant, but became aware immediately that I had one more piece than I was allowed. He had not yet lifted or weighed each one, and I knew without his telling me what problem that was going to be. He started to comment on the fact that internationally only four bags are allowed without additional charges. Then the door to the baggage area opened and out walked Dave Paquette!

Dave said to the clerk who was waiting on me, "I'll help you check the bags in." He lifted the first one, winced and said without putting it on the scales, "I think this one will do, even though it feels a bit heavy." On the next one he frowned, but avoiding the scales asked only, "What do you have in these bags?"

"Gifts for the missionaries and things they cannot get in Ecuador," I said.

He did the same with the fifth bag, and the other clerk said not a word! He had heard about the reason for the extra weight and the extra bag, and he used his own judgment and let it slide by. The bags were checked right through to Quito, so there was no further problem to worry about.

Once again the Lord had taken care of the overweight problem, even though at first my specific prayer, *Let Dave be the one to check us in*, seemed to have been unheard and unanswered.

There Is Nothing He Cannot Do!

1992

What a shock to receive that late evening phone call from the oncologist! He said the X ray taken earlier in the day had revealed that the cancer had affected my honey's hip so extensively that it was in imminent danger of breaking. A walker and a wheelchair were to be used at all times and the first of twenty-two treatments of radiation would be started immediately.

We stopped to price walkers and wheelchairs. They were asking nearly $70 for a walker and $500 for a wheelchair! The doctor had said that after the radiation treatments the hip might recalcify and in about three months after that she might be able to put weight on that hip again. So the need could possibly be a temporary one. What should we do? We priced what it would cost to rent a wheelchair. They wanted $52 a month to rent one. That would be $208 for the four months we might be needing it!

I called my brother, David, to see if my mother was still using the wheelchair she had gotten from my cousin.

"Yes, they are getting her up in it daily," he said. But he made a suggestion I had never even thought of: "Have you called your local rescue squad? Here in New Jersey we loan that kind of equipment out." He even phoned down to Tennessee, for he is one of the volunteers there, and he felt free to ask them about it. They told him they did have a wheelchair, but no walker. Of the two, the wheelchair was preferable anyway, because the walker could be gotten for $70. We praised the Lord for providing the larger piece of equipment.

That very day we had to leave for Raleigh, North Carolina for a weekend of meetings at the Alliance Church where Elaine's cousin, Arlie McGarvey, was pastoring. While we were there he told us about Mittie Chisenhall, a lady in his congregation who owned a medical supply store. He told us what a dedicated Christian widow she was, having raised her four children alone after her husband died. She had first worked at the store, and then had purchased it to operate herself!

He spoke to her about our need for a walker. When we came back to the parsonage, there sat a beautiful new one by the side door. I tried to pay for it on Sunday, but she said that she doesn't do any business on Sunday. I assured her we would get a check off to her as soon as the bill came. She would not even tell me the price. A month later we learned that we would never be receiving a bill; it was her gift to us!

We saw it as God's gift to us as well. God knows the location of everything we need, including wheelchairs and walkers. An old hymn by Oswald J. Smith and Bentley D. Ackley says it clearly: "The Saviour can solve every problem."

"He who did not spare his own Son, but gave him up for us all—how will he not also, along with him, graciously give us all things?" (Romans 8:32).

First-Class Citizens

1992

*T*he twenty-two radiation treatments were half completed. The oncologist had said they were necessary to kill the pain and stop the tumor from totally destroying Elaine's hip and femur. She was confined to a wheelchair.

They had told us to expect certain side effects which were enough to prevent us from making the trip to Vancouver to attend the annual Fairhaven banquet in that city. We were pleased that so far there was no evidence of side effects except for fatigue. That could be handled easily by taking naps a couple of times a day.

I called to get our seat assignments for the four flights. The reservations had been made much earlier, but USAir did not give seat assignments until twenty-one days before departure. I delayed one day because of a busy schedule of my own, and on the twentieth day before our departure I made the call.

To my surprise and distress, one of the four flights was already almost completely assigned. The only seats remaining were in row fifteen or at the very end of the plane. Because of the nature of the possible side effects, there was nothing we could do but to take seats at the rear of the plane, where there would be bathrooms. I felt angry with myself for not having called twenty-four hours earlier, for I knew it would distress my honey to be carried the whole length of the plane like that, twice!

I was requesting to-the-seat wheelchair assistance because Elaine was not allowed to place any weight on that hip. I phoned our special Christian friend Dave Paquette out at our airport to see if there might be a waiting list we could go on in hopes of getting better seats because of cancellations or other changes. He was off for a few days, so I wrote a letter that would be waiting for him when he returned to the USAir counter.

I was so desperate for better seats that I even asked whether we could upgrade to first class for that one long leg of the trip. I told him I realized that traveling as we were on senior coupons, it was probably an impossibility. (We would be going round-trip coast-to-coast for less than $200 each on those coupons.)

A few days later Mr. Paquette phoned. "Your letter was here waiting for me when I got back," he said. "We can help! USAir is a very compassionate airline. I took your letter to my boss and we decided together to upgrade you to first class for the entire trip, compliments of USAir."

Yes, "all things" do work together for our good, for we do love the Lord and have been called according to His purposes. Even my delay until all good seats were gone was in His plan. I would not have written such a letter of inquiry if they had offered us acceptable seats in economy class on all four flights.

In the midst of the radiation treatments, that serendipity provided a burst of sunshine that lifted our spirits wonderfully. God made clear to us that when He wants His servants to go "first class," He knows how to take care of that.

Your Joy Will Be Complete

1992

*O*h, how we enjoyed those dark blue leather seats! They were so wide and comfortable, with legroom enough for a basketball player. What a contrast it was to the way we usually flew, back there in economy class!

My heart was filled with praise to the Lord for making these first-class accommodations available to us on senior coupons. We were actually flying coast-to-coast round-trip for less than $200 each in first class. I felt like we were dreaming!

The across-the-United-States flight was long, giving us plenty of time to read, sleep, pray and think. My thoughts turned to our arrival in Seattle. I rehearsed the routine: 1) get a USAir wheelchair for Elaine; 2) wait for the baggage to come on the carousel; 3) go for the rental car while she sits in the USAir wheelchair; 4) return for Elaine in the subcompact car we had ordered for only $89.95 for the whole week!

Subcompact! Did I order a subcompact?

Suddenly the realization flooded over me that a wheelchair probably would not fit in the trunk of that kind of car! A Geo Storm or a Colt or something similar was what they had promised. They are nice, but they are also really small. What can you expect for only $12.50 a day?

Lord Jesus, I prayed, *please let them upgrade us from a small car to a midsized car*. I didn't stop to think

211

about the audacity of such a prayer! I was sitting in leather first-class seats and *asking for more!* Well, I just had a deep sense of being His child, loved by Him and felt free to ask, that's all.

At the General Car Rental lot, the clerk began picking at car key possibilities and glancing out the windows at the cars in the lot.

I spoke up. "In the category we have reserved, if there is any choice at all, I would appreciate the one with the biggest trunk as I have a wheelchair to try to get in it."

"Come along with me," the man said, "and we will look at them together."

As we walked out into the lot he continued, "For only a few dollars a day I could upgrade you to a full-size car like a Dynasty, or similar."

"That's very tempting," I replied, "but my wife is having twenty-two very expensive radiation treatments for cancer and we have no medical insurance, so I think we had better try to manage with the subcompact."

We were walking past the luxury cars now. Suddenly he slapped the hood of a pure white Chrysler New Yorker with a deep red interior. "I think I'll put you in this one, and it is our gift to you. Take it and have a wonderful trip!"

I later learned that it rented for $50 a day! We had been upgraded *four* categories! I nearly cried! In fact, I actually hugged him—a perfect stranger—right there in the parking lot. After a prayer of thanksgiving I drove back to the airport to get Elaine. I did cry a little along the way, my heart was so full of praise and joy. "Ask and you will receive, and your joy will be complete" (John 16:24).

1992

*T*he annual General Ministerial Convention for the Churches of Christ in Christian Union finished at noon, June 3. Elaine and I left Circleville, Ohio rejoicing over how well the ministry to those pastors and their wives had been received. It had been a much bigger convention than I had anticipated. Now, at last, we were able to relax.

The trip had been a full one. It had begun with autographing copies of my new book, *A Heart for Imbabura*, at the General Council of The Christian and Missionary Alliance in Lexington, Kentucky. From there we had hurried on up to Mansfield, Ohio to speak at the commencement exercises of the Mansfield Christian School. We traveled on from there to the convention in Circleville. Now all that was history.

We could have driven all the way home in seven hours, but we felt the need of traveling slowly, stopping a lot and enjoying ourselves, since the tensions of ministry were behind us. We found a pretty blouse and jacket for Elaine. I found a beautiful summer shirt and a priced-right belt for me.

Then we decided it was time to begin to look for our motel for the night. The first one we tried was full. Next I found one that had just one room left on the first floor, but it was right beside the ice machine, and we knew better than to take that one. We had suffered through an experience like that once and had determined never to do that again.

A mile away there was a nice one with acceptable prices, but I would have had to carry everything in through the vestibule and down a long hall to get to the inside door. We like better the motels where you can park right by the door and easily unload.

The next motel was a Holiday Inn and much too expensive. Soon after that we came to a Super 8. It was a little bit high-priced, but very nice. We almost took it. Later in the evening I would come to the conclusion that the decision not to take it was a big mistake, for we never found one as nice for as good a price.

Since it wasn't really terribly late, we decided to check out another one on down the road. That one had the right price and the room was clean, but it was eight miles from any eating place. We had not had our supper yet. That would mean sixteen miles round trip to get something to eat. The next one was dirty! Then there was another one that was too expensive and still another one not really clean enough.

Checking out all those places had consumed a lot of time, and we were getting closer and closer to home. We had stopped to eat as well, and now it was getting on past 10 o'clock. We figured that we could be home in our own bed by 12:30 a.m., but we were really tired by now and didn't relish that. However, there didn't seem to be any choice, for we were encountering no towns or motels now.

Suddenly we passed the Carriage Hill Motel. It had a "Mom and Pop" look to it. Sometimes that kind of motel is very acceptable, and sometimes not at all. In the darkness we couldn't really tell too much about it with any certainty. We almost decided not to stop, and drove right past it, but then I made a U-turn, and we went back to check it out.

The lady quoted me a price that was very reasonable, but said that price was for only one bed. "Two beds are $36," she said.

I told her that with Elaine's cancer, we usually liked to get two beds, as she slept better in her own bed.

The lady's eyes filled with tears as she offered me the two-bed room for $32. "My husband died of cancer two months ago," she confided. She talked with me so long about her loneliness and how difficult it was for her, that Elaine wondered what was keeping me.

God had directed our paths to someone who needed a word of comfort and encouragement. In the morning we tried to see her to bring more encouragement to her, but she was away from the motel when we got up late. So I wrote a letter to Lois Bolling and sent her *Our Daily Bread*.

I know now why it was so hard for us to make up our mind. God had someone on down the road that He wanted us to meet, so He closed door after door (in our own minds, at least) to keep us traveling on to the right spot. We must always remember that God is often in our disappointing turns of events, and even develop an attitude of expectation when things happen like that.

God, the Interior Decorator

1993

*I*t was not easy to get excited about the holiday season when cancer was taking a ravaging toll and threatening to make the Christmas of 1993 the saddest one we had ever known. In fact, I almost stopped by the funeral parlor to discuss some things with the undertaker but couldn't quite bring myself to do it. Elaine, though not bedfast yet, was so bad that not even doubling the morphine relieved her of the intense pain she was suffering. We both realized she was nearing the end of her days.

Elaine was crying out with pain at about fifteen minute intervals all through the night. I was so weary from lack of sleep that I was afraid I might go down physically too.

Decorate the house for Christmas? How? With what energy? All my energy was being expended in caring for my sweetheart and trying to keep up with the Fairhaven mail as well as meals, housekeeping and other chores.

My grandchildren were in the play *The Best Christmas Ever* way down in Mongayacu, Ecuador near their home in Shell. I prayed earnestly, *Lord, You know how much it means to them to be in that play! Please don't let me have to call and ask them to come home before that exciting night!*

Decorations? While I had no energy left to get them out and put them up, I knew it would cheer us both to see some of the red and green and the beauty of Christmas around the house.

God knew it too. He had already made His plans. The doorbell rang, and the most beautiful Christmas arrangement we had seen in a long time was delivered. "From Pauline," the card read. That would be Pauline Myers, up in Ohio, a dear friend of ours. The arrangement was *exquisite*!

That was the beginning of our Christmas decorations. But that was only the beginning. Our faithful Fairhaven staff brought a beautiful, large, deep red poinsettia—it was about the prettiest poinsettia I had ever seen, and it added a lot to our Christmas cheer.

Then came another "ding-dong" of our doorbell a day or so later. This poinsettia was the fullest, largest one I had ever seen in all my life. It was mammoth! The card read, "Ben Whittemore."

"Who is Ben Whittemore?" I asked Elaine.

She thought for a moment and then said, "I think it is that new man who sits in front of us at our church."

She was right. He was brand new to our church and yet he sent this marvelous Christmas ornamentation to us. "On the fourth day of Christmas" the doorbell rang again. Two flower arrangements! One was unique. The basket was very large. On one side of the handle was a full poinsettia plant. It was placed in the basket in such a manner that you couldn't see the pot, for it was surrounded by cascading holly-imprinted ribbon. The other side of the basket had an arrangement of white chrysanthemums and pine boughs. The blend of red, white and green was gorgeous! Again the card read, "Pauline"! What a special friend!

The other bouquet was a stately arrangement of scotch pine, white pine, red and white carnations and three tall, slender, red candles, all in a gorgeous red metallic oval-shaped base. The card read, "Glen and Priscilla." It had come from one of Canada's finest organists, Glen Hoskyn and his beloved wife, who used to be a part of the Billy Graham trio. They were very special people who were going through traumatic physical testings themselves. Yet they thought of us!

That night I set the table with some deep red Christmas place mats, clear glass plates and crystal goblets, and lit some additional candles so as not to spoil the ones in the formal centerpiece. We ate by candlelight from plates on which I had carefully arranged the food in gourmet style, so I could invite Elaine to the candlelit dining room, with a white towel over my arm, pretending to be a waiter in the elegant El Jardin restaurant there in Quenca, Ecuador—a happy memory from one of our trips down to see our little family serving there.

Our house had never seen such luxurious Christmas decorations, and all because of loving friends the Lord had prompted to decorate for us when we had no energies left to do it ourselves. I thought of the chorus of a hymn that says, "Oh, yes, He cares; I know He cares, His heart is touched with [our] grief." (*Does Jesus Care?* by Frank E. Graeff and J. Lincoln Hall.)

I will always remember the Christmas when God decorated our house for us, and how He touched Elaine and raised her up again briefly, so we could go on a little Christmas mini-trip I had planned. But that's another story.

For This I Have Jesus

1993

Saturday, August 28th, 1993 brought the usual batch of mail to be processed. I sorted it into Fairhaven Ministries business and the personal items which almost always included encouragement cards for Elaine and me. That day there were a number of such encouragements, but none bigger than the two that came that day. Let me tell you about them separately. The first one came from Gordon and Janis Timyan, former missionaries to Africa, living in retirement in Jacksonville, Florida. They sent a very nice note in which they had enclosed a small pamphlet. I quote the entire text of it here:

For This I Have Jesus

Many years ago in a small church in Ireland a message was given in which the minister said that Jesus' words, "Abide in me, and I in you," mean to simply say in every circumstance, "For this I have Jesus" and Jesus will say, "For this you have Me."

While he was speaking, a telegram was delivered to the young pianist. It read: "Mother very ill. Take first train home." At the conclusion of the message she shared the telegram with the congregation, and she added: "I have never traveled alone, but 'For this I have Jesus.' I must take a midnight train, but 'For this I have Jesus.' Then I take a long train trip to the south of England, but 'For this' and all the suspense along the way, 'I have Jesus.' "

As she spoke these words, we saw the light of heaven on her face.

Several weeks later a letter came from her which was a song of praise. She wrote, "As I traveled that long sorrowful journey, I continued to say, 'For this I have Jesus' and He answered, 'For this you have Me.' "

When I reached home, my sister fell sobbing on my shoulder saying, "Oh, if you had come ten minutes sooner you would have seen Mother who so longed to see you."

Instantly I looked up and said, "For this I have Jesus," and He came between me and my sorrow, and vain regrets had no power over me.

We had never had a death or funeral in our family, and they all depended on me for every decision. Acknowledging my ignorance, I said softly, "For this I have Jesus," and He gave His wisdom for every detail. There was also His perfect peace for all legal matters that needed attention. Now life has become joyous and victorious as in every circumstance I continue to say, "For this I have Jesus.' "

. . . What is the circumstance in your life today that is beyond your control? Is it sorrow, sickness, suffering, fear, unsaved relatives, disappointment, discouragement, guidance, finances, misunderstanding or another trial? You also can look into His face and say, "For this I have Jesus," and He will say, "For this you have Me."

The contents of that pamphlet by itself were a big encouragement to Elaine and me, but God had an even bigger one ahead! As we continued to open the mail, we came to a card that had been in the mail for awhile, for it had come all the way from Richmond, British Columbia, Canada. It was from Mr. and Mrs. Alfred Barber, friends and former parishioners. Their beautiful little card had a few words of encouragement and appreciation. Enclosed was the following note: "It's so wonderful to know that, for all this rough passage, 'you have Jesus.' "

Can you imagine how thrilled we were to have the Lord confirm to our hearts that the thought "For this I have Jesus" had come from God Himself to us through the Timyans and the Barbers? He was making very clear to us again that He is in complete control, even of the Canadian and U.S. mail systems (and that is really going some!).

Once again that was not all! I wrote back to Mrs. Barber and to the Timyans. I asked Dorothy Barber if she had seen that tract.

Dorothy wrote in answer, "When I was writing that last note, I asked Alf if he had heard or seen that phrase. Yes, he had but he didn't know where, so I just felt that God gave it to me at that moment to pass on to you."

I am so certain He did!

Whatever you face in your lifetime, always remember, "For this you have Jesus!"

A House Call!

1993

*D*octors don't make house calls anymore. In fact, the doctor who had been so kind as to write prescriptions for painkillers and sedatives had office hours Monday through Friday from 9 to 5. So why did the drastic turn for the worse in Elaine have to come on a Saturday morning?

The sedative I had given her on Friday evening should have kept her under its effect until noon, but by 8:30 a.m. on the monitor downstairs in my office, I could hear her moaning. I hurried up to her hospital bed in our bedroom. She was writhing in pain. Elaine cried out with pain as I helped her up and supported her for those few short steps into the adjacent bathroom. She was hurting so badly. Another rib must have broken. Even a deep breath would cause her to cry out with pain. She readily agreed to my increasing the dosage of painkiller for the fourth time in less than a month, and even swallowed another Ativan (a sedative), knowing it would probably put her out for the entire day. I rubbed her back and comforted her for nearly an hour, until the two medications had taken effect and she was asleep. Then I went down to my office and sat there feeling terribly alone. Our doctor was not available unless I called him at home. I hated to do that.

The phone rang. It was Paul Branch from the Boone Alliance Bible Fellowship. But wait a minute. I need to back up a bit and tell you about something that happened late in the afternoon of the preceding day. The phone had rung then, too.

It was Roy King, the Pastor of the Alliance Bible Fellowship over in Boone, North Carolina. He told me the board had met the night before and had specifically asked him to phone me to learn the latest on how Elaine was. He said they wanted us to know that the church stood ready to do anything at all they could to help us. Was there anything we needed?

"Yes," I replied. "In your church you have Wanda Branch who is the head of the HOSPICE program for your area. If she would ever be coming over toward Elizabethton, we would deeply appreciate it if she could stop by our home unofficially to answer a few questions for us."

He told me that Mr. and Mrs. Branch came to Elizabethton regularly and that he would arrange with them to stop by sometime. Paul Branch was an owner of the pharmacy located in the Cannon Memorial Hospital over in Banner Elk, North Carolina. His wife Wanda was the head of the HOSPICE program for three North Carolina counties.

So, as I said, the call that Saturday morning was from Paul Branch. He asked if it would be convenient for him and his wife and Dr. Peter Haibach to come to our home that afternoon! Dr. Haibach was the doctor who had originally diagnosed Elaine's cancer many years earlier. He is also a member of the Boone Fellowship. A Christian doctor would be coming all the way from North Carolina to make a house call! With him would be a pharmacist and the head of an extensive HOSPICE program! That meant that three very fine Christian professionals would be coming to our door just when we needed them most.

Suddenly I did not feel "alone" at all. I recognized that my heavenly Father knew exactly what both Elaine and I needed so desperately, and in a country where no doctors make house calls, even in town, He sent one from another state!

Dr. Haibach gave Elaine a thorough examination. He said that she had broken two ribs this time! He felt it was time to start on morphine, but Elaine had felt that was the end of the line. While Paul Branch was filling Dr. Haibach's prescription in the living room out of the satchel full of medications he had brought along, Wanda Branch sat on Elaine's bed and convinced her that morphine was not the end of the line. She even told her that the addiction could be broken rather quickly if she were to improve.

A day that had begun as one of the worst days of our lives, God turned into a special day in which His meticulous planning could be clearly revealed.

Postscript: When I opened my Bible for my personal devotions the next morning, the first thing I saw in my NIV Bible was a paragraph heading in Genesis 18 that made the goosebumps come out on me! It read: "The Three Visitors," referring to the three who appeared to Abraham.

How Very Nice of Him!

1994

*I*t is impossible to convey to you fully how traumatic it was for me when the cancer took my sweetheart's ability to reason and converse away from her. Elaine no longer knew who I was. She called me "Mister" when she wanted water. Sometimes she was even afraid of me, afraid I was trying to kill her with the morphine I wanted to give her to conquer the pain. If she did say a name, it was "Elwood." All men, except me, had become "Elwood," her brother's name; I was always "Mister." All women had become "Pauline," a good friend.

My heart was deeply grieved over the loss of my honey. Her body was still alive, but her brain was being destroyed by the cancer.

After church early one Sunday afternoon, Dr. and Mrs. Moyer who are on our Fairhaven staff stopped by to visit with us. They went in Elaine's room and Stan offered prayer for her. She looked up at him with a somewhat blank stare and said, "Elwood!"

As they left our home, Stan slipped a note into my hand. I read it right after they left. *I am praying that God will give Elaine a moment of sanity so you can have some meaningful time together once more before He takes her home.*

225

I was deeply touched by the fact that he cared about my heartache. *How nice of him!* I thought. I have to confess that I had no faith to believe that such an audacious prayer would ever be answered. My faith had reached a pretty low ebb, to tell the truth!

Can you imagine how startled I was the next evening when I slipped into Elaine's room and saw her smile at me and heard her say, "I just love this time of night!"

"You do, sweetheart! Why?" I blurted out in unbridled astonishment.

"Because it is a time when you and I can just talk together," she said so sweetly, almost nostalgically.

"Oh, my darling, what would you like to talk about?" I exclaimed, as I pulled a chair over to the side of her bed. I was utterly amazed!

She grinned and said, "As long as I can't do a thing to help you anymore, why don't I just make some more work for you?"

Her old sense of humor was back!

We chuckled together over that one.

"What would you like me to do, honey?" I asked.

"Please get some paper. I want to write a little note to some of those who have meant so much to me during my lifetime."

I quickly got a legal pad and pen and she began to dictate the sweetest little notes. I was thrilled!

Then she said, "I'd like to write one to you too, honey, but I could never tell you how much you mean to me and how much I appreciate the way you have cared for me!"

"You don't need to, sweetheart," I reassured her. "I already know."

Then she sighed, and said with a thinning voice, "I'm getting tired."

I felt I might lose her again soon, so I said quickly, "Sweetheart, let me have prayer with you." I put my left hand on her right cheek gently, because the doctor had said her neck could break at any time. I put my left cheek against her left one, and I prayed for the darling of my heart.

When I finished my brief prayer, to my amazement she started to pray. I will *never* forget that prayer! "Dear Jesus, I don't understand why You don't take me home, like I have been asking You to, but I want to be faithful to the very end. And when I'm gone, would You please take care of my honey . . . and help him to . . . help . . . him . . . to . . ." Here she gave a big sigh, and then continued more weakly. "Help him to look both ways . . . before he crosses the street."

She was gone from me now. It was "Mister, water!" again.

That precious, precious time together was the last I ever had with Elaine. I thank God for letting me enjoy that with her. And I thank Stan for having faith that I did not have to ask God for a miracle of no small proportion! How very nice of him, and of Him!

God Can "Transform" Anything

1994

$\mathcal{E}$laine was very ill with cancer. I knew that it would take her life unless God chose to work a miracle. It was difficult to watch her life slowly ebb away.

Satan tried to add all kinds of other difficulties to the burden I was carrying. I knew where the lies were coming from, but it was difficult to combat them because my energies had been sapped. I really needed the prayers of others. We both did!

One of the lies Satan whispered in my ear was that my ministry was finished. I knew all God expected from me was faithfulness in ministering to one of His very choice servants, and that He was pleased with me for doing my very best for her. But I couldn't escape the fact that I was no longer preaching and I had canceled 150 meetings. Such a significant series as a citywide campaign for The Christian and Missionary Alliance Churches of Lincoln, Nebraska was among those I had regrettably canceled, knowing I was doing the right thing before the Lord and by my sweetheart.

It was on February 6 that I prayed, *Will I ever again be taken off the shelf, Lord? Please reassure me that I will still have a preaching ministry after we have emerged from this "valley of the shadow of death."*

The very next day a letter came from one of America's great radio preachers, Ord Morrow. The letter was used of God to help me keep things in perspective. This is how it read:

I do not expect you to remember me. We have met only in passing a couple of times across the years. *[What humility! He was the main speaker on the Back to the Bible Broadcast. Certainly I knew of him and admired him.]* My son Roger knows you from St. Paul Bible College and often speaks of you with high praise and appreciation.

I attend Old Cheney Alliance Church here in Lincoln and attend the monthly meeting of the C.M.A. pastors. I was sorry to hear that you must cancel your being with us in meetings. Of course we understand and feel you made the right decision. I personally felt God might use you in a large way here in Lincoln. He knows best, and we do not question His ways.

Nearly two years ago I had serious back surgery. I am still in therapy and have a lot of time to just think. You and your wife have been in mind many times and we (all the ministers) pray for you. My therapy calls for a lot of walking. I have a treadmill, since walking outside is generally not possible in our part of the country. I started to listen to tapes as I walk. I have had dozens given to me across the years. Recently it was my "hap" to find one of yours sent out by TRANSFORMATION TAPES. It was a message on prayer. My, what a blessing that message was to me! I have listened three times. I finally decided I would use some of the ideas for prayer meeting. But since the prayer group is small,

> I decided to use the whole tape in the adult Sunday school class at Old Cheney.
>
> Sorry it has taken me so long to get to the point. I just thought I must write and tell you your ministry continues to be a blessing to many places and people, even when you do not know it.

Remember, my prayer for reassurance was February 6. The letter quoted above arrived on February 7. That same day a letter came from David Presher, the District Superintendent of the Ohio Valley District. It was an invitation to speak at a districtwide conference for a week in 1995. On the eighth a letter came from the Churches of Christ in Christian Union asking if I would be the main speaker at their denomination's annual gathering in 1995. On the ninth an invitation came from Pastor Grumbine in Maine asking if I would minister for a week in his church and the church in Cosco, Maine. Four invitations had come, plus this very kind letter of reminder that even now (not in the future) I had a ministry that extended beyond the little bedroom where my precious Elaine was needing my careful attention and love.

God was not through with me yet, and He made that crystal clear. He used a TRANSFORMATION TAPE and a great preacher to remind me that He cares about what we are thinking, and especially about what we pray, when we are honest with Him about our fears and our feelings. He transformed my own attitudes, delivering me from my fears and offering me reassurances so very graciously and sweetly.

God called Elaine "Home" on May 19, 1994.

In the evening, on the final day of Elaine's life, my son Brian and his wife Connie, my son Gary my sister-in-law Dorothy and I stood around her bed singing her into heaven. Unexpectedly she came out of her coma, opened her eyes looked at each of us, closed her eyes, and never breathed again. Brian broke into song and we all joined him in singing *Praise God from whom all blessings flow*. It was all over now. God had gently led Elaine safely "home."

After calling Elaine to Himself, God opened doors beyond my greatest expectations. In the first twelve months following her death, I ministered in six different countries. I did not count the number of times I spoke in that year, but I am certain they exceeded the number I had canceled during the time Elaine and I were confined together.

God was not through with me, though the enemy would have liked me to believe that lie. I could not know ahead of time what God planned for me, so He brought me the encouragement and reassurance I needed right then through that special letter from Ord Morrow and the invitations that followed day after day. God's tender love for us is beautiful to behold!

You Have Not Because You Ask Not

1994

I had just completed with God's blessing a half-week of meetings in Sebring, Florida. Pastor Jim O'Hara had driven me over to Shell Point Village to spend a couple of days as the guest of the director, Peter Dys, before heading back home. I thoroughly enjoyed looking around the beautifully manicured village and stopping by the site where Sundial would be built. I tried to imagine how much pleasure I would get out of living in one of those brand new apartments in that high-rise. The one I had chosen would look right out on the marina.

Now, as I sat in my motel room on the island, reflecting upon the pleasures of those two days, I realized that I had felt somewhat alone at times, not having sufficient friends to meet my need for close friendship. I reflected upon the fact that one of my best friends, Leon Bowman, and his wife Arlys would almost certainly never come to Shell Point Village since they had children in Minnesota, and that would be so far away from them. What would I do for close friendships? I told myself that when the time came, I could surely find someone among the 1,200 residents whom I would enjoy knowing and with whom it would be a pleasure to develop a close relationship.

It had been nice of Rosalys Tyler to invite me over for dinner, but she was a widow, and there would have to be a limited amount of such socializing since I had no intention whatsoever of close relationships with other women. Elaine was still the darling of my heart, even though she had been seven months in heaven now.

Lord Jesus, I know You could send me a friend. When the time comes to move in, I could just ask You to do that. You could even help me to find another man who is in a similar situation to my own. I know that. In my prayer, I meant two years on down the road, when I would move in. I never dreamed He planned to answer so swiftly.

I had brought with me 139 letters that needed to be answered on my new laptop. At Sebring and then at Shell Point Village I had completed 135. I picked up number 136 and could hardly believe my eyes! This is how part of it read:

> Dear Dr. Shepson:
>
> Although we have never met, I feel a deep kinship with you. Dr. Gilbert Johnson and his wife Ida have been close friends since the days that he did such a super job of teaching at Shell Point Village.
>
> Their love and concern deepened when Florence, my loving wife of fifty-eight years died on April 19, 1994 just one month exactly before Elaine joined the Savior.
>
> The Johnsons have shared your deep Christian commitment with me. My closest relatives are a daughter in California and a son in Colorado, so I don't see them very often. In 1976 we were led to spend the winters in Fort Myers and bought a resi-

dence in Palm Acres (that's right across the canal from the Village). I have now decided to sell and to move into Shell Point Village.

There is good reason to believe we could be a source of comfort and encouragement to one another as we seek to reflect our Christian faith in adjusting to a solitary lifestyle.

Since you plan to be in Fort Myers on December 15 and 16, perhaps we could meet and spend a few minutes together at your convenience.

Your Christian brother,
Ted Blake

I sat stunned! God had heard my prayer and answered *immediately*! I picked up the phone in the motel room and called the number on Ted's letterhead, and within ten minutes he had ridden his bicycle over to the motel and we were sitting together sharing our sweet memories of the sweethearts that had meant so much to us. I found him to be a most pleasant, very young in spirit, intelligent man (a former executive in a large bank in Cleveland, Ohio). We had a wonderful hour of sharing together and then praying together. We hugged each other warmly as we separated, looking forward to the further development of our friendship when we would both move into the Village.

1995-1996

*. . . weeping may remain for a night, but rejoic-
ing comes in the morning.*
(Psalm 30:5)

Perfect Timing

1995

How nice of the DeGarises and the Grahams to treat me to Sunday dinner at Makato's in Johnson City! It was fun watching the Japanese cook prepare the meal right there in front of us.

Going out with them helped take my mind off my troubles. The accident five days earlier when I had slammed into a spinning, out-of-control car had been such a big loss to me. Now I had a rental car to drive, and it had high mileage.

That concerned me, for they said they didn't want me to take the car out of the area. My book, *Hidden Manna*, was ready to be picked up. I had planned to pull a trailer to Toccoa Falls Press to pick up the fifty boxes of books. Now that plan was defunct!

For the moment that was all forgotten as I enjoyed the fellowship with those two couples. Even the trip back to Elizabethton was pleasant. They dropped me off right near my rental car.

That's where the special intervention of God stepped in. I didn't notice the pile of mail on the seat next to me as I started home. After about seven blocks, I suddenly realized that I had planned to drop those letters in the post office while downtown. It provoked me that I could be so forgetful. *Should I go back to the post office or just forget it?* I wondered.

My decision was to go for it. So I headed back to the post office, feeling a bit frustrated and never dreaming that this was the Lord's doing. No one was in the lobby on a Sunday afternoon as I went inside and dropped the mail in the slot and left. I had to wait for a pickup truck to pass where I was parked so I could back out. It pulled in a few spaces on past me.

The man who stepped out waved to me. I waved back and then realized it was a special friend of mine. I pulled back in and got out to greet him.

"Come on into the lobby with me," he suggested. It was warmer there.

"I have had you specially on my heart both yester-day and today!" he exclaimed. "What's happening?"

I told him all I have already told you.

"You must not make that long drive to Toccoa," he practically commanded! "I want you to have them shipped right here to Elizabethton, and I will pay for the shipping." He was insistent.

What a burden that took off my shoulders! It also freed me up for an additional day in the office trying to catch up on things.

God knew exactly when to have me make that U-turn so that Frank Schaff and I would end up at the post office at the same time. His timing is perfect, *always*! He knows everything that concerns us, and He lovingly concerns Himself with those same things, working out *His* perfect plan to cope with those problems. How very special it is to be special to Him!

Jehovah-Rapha

1995

*I*t will help you to understand the reason for the title of this chapter if I interpret the words for you. God gave to Himself seven compound names that begin with Jehovah. This particular one means, "The Lord who Heals" or "The Lord, your Physician."

It was on January 6, 1995 that I started the new year off with an unwelcome bang! I was traveling up into Ohio headed for Akron. The ice storm the weather channel had predicted turned out to be much worse than I had expected. After only thirty minutes of driving, a freezing rain began and I headed into the worst ice storm of my life. The car was covered with a layer of ice anywhere from a half an inch to two inches thick! There were wrecks everywhere, including an overturned car. I went off the road four times and finally decided to call it a halt and get a motel. I could find only one and it was sleazy. So I kept going, risking my life, actually!

When I pulled in at the Knight's Inn in Washington Court House, Ohio, where I was to stay for the next five days, I breathed a sigh of relief and thanked the Lord for His protection. But I was hungry, so I decided to go next door to get something to eat. That proved to be my downfall, *literally*! The grocery store had put out "ice melt" and their sidewalk was safe, but

The Fashion Bug had not. Their "60% off" sign in the window lured me. I love a bargain!

This proved to be no bargain, however, for when I stepped up onto their curb, I was down in an instant on the sidewalk, and my wrist hurt something fierce! I went inside to tell them about it and to ask them to put some ice melt out so no one else would have such a bad fall. I could wiggle my fingers, and even rotate my wrist somewhat, so I disdained going to the hospital emergency room. I got some food at the grocery store and went back to my room to eat it. But I could not even take my coat off. The man in the next room had to do that for me. And when I dressed to go to the church service where I was to speak, I had to ask someone to button the top button on my shirt and to tie my shoes. I could do neither!

After three weeks of having people astounded that I was not having it x-rayed, I finally went to a doctor who looked at it, twisted it a little and nearly sent me through the roof with pain when he rotated it in a certain direction.

"Yep! It's a break all right, but that kind of break we usually just put in splints. You just keep it bandaged with an ace bandage (which I had been doing), and I think it will be OK." He explained that the bone I had broken was "the little one that is by that bump on your wrist," and that I should perhaps even cushion it. He didn't x-ray it!

So, for the next three weeks I heard the rebukes of people who learned how severe my pain was in that wrist, and who felt I was just being foolish by not getting an X ray. I realized they could be right. Then I learned that my brother David had just had surgery for a similar injury that was many months old. His pain had never gone away, either. I became more than a little concerned. The doctor operated for two and one-half hours on him, removing a splinter of bone when he finally found it.

So I made an appointment with an orthopedic surgeon over in Boone, North Carolina. On February 17, six weeks to the day from my fall on the ice, I had Dr. Kadyk examine my wrist.

He ordered three X rays of different angles of the wrist. Then he showed them to me and to his nurse. "See, here is a break all the way across the larger bone and here is another in the small bone. If you had come to me when it first happened, I would have had to put it in splints so you would not do further damage to it. But look, it is healing perfectly! You haven't done it any damage at all. You won't even need to come back to see me. The pain will continue to abate slowly. You may suffer for a few more months."

His nurse told me on the side, "That has to be the Lord!"

Yes, it *was* the Lord. I *know* it was! I went out to the car and sat there crying for awhile, repeating over and over these words: "The best possible news! The best possible news!" I really needed that uplift, for I had ruined my beautiful car just the week before on ice and was driving a clunker now temporarily, and it seemed like so many things had gone wrong. So over and over and over I found myself saying aloud, "The best possible news!" as I headed home.

I pulled into the Wendy's parking lot to treat myself to a Frosty. As I stepped out of the car and headed across the parking lot, I said right out loud once again, "The best possible news!" And then it happened! I saw right before my eyes on the side of a van parked at an angle, the phrase, "The best news in all the world!"

I gasped! I had never seen those words on a van before. That van was all the way from Anniston, Alabama, two states away, and here it was parked in Boone, North Carolina, for me! It was from the Saks Baptist Church and had probably brought a group of young people to Boone to ski.

To me it was God Himself letting me know that He had heard my note of praise so oft repeated: *The best possible news!* He had seen my tears of joy. How thrilled my heart was to rejoice in the truth that "The Lord my Physician" (Jehovah-Rapha) had cared for those two breaks in His own special and tender way, perhaps even putting on His own invisible splints! The icing on the cake, however, was that God said, "*I hear you!*" when I repeatedly and thankfully said, "The best possible news!"

Happy Anniversary!

1995

*I*f there was ever a day that I would not expect to be happy, this would be it. *How will I handle the first anniversary of Elaine's death?* I wondered.

My emotions had been rather fragile all week. Soon I would be flying to Japan and Guam on a two-week mission. One doctor was even concerned that I might be in mild depression and prescribed an antidepressant for me. Another doctor said he disagreed; the anniversary of the death of someone as dearly loved as my wife had been was a time when it was quite normal to be having a resurgence of grief, he insisted.

As I contemplated the tour and especially the date, May 19, I realized that I would have very heavy responsibilities. I would minister in the afternoon to a group of Japanese pastors through an interpreter. In the evening their thirteen churches would be combining in the central church in downtown Tokyo, where I would be speaking again.

When the nineteenth rolled around, I was thrilled to be ministering to those respectful Japanese people. My pure white hair contributed to how deeply they honored me. They revere old age.

In that evening service, I preached a sermon entitled, "The Ultimate Intimacy." One of the illustrations I use early in that sermon describes vividly the last moments of Elaine's life. Because of preaching through an interpreter and concentrating on making each sentence crystal clear, I was able to tell it all without breaking down. The sermon went very well, under the Lord's blessing.

Near the end of the service, I told how fitting it seemed to me to be preaching on this special subject on this particular day. I told them that Elaine had grieved over my not being able to go out preaching while I was housebound taking care of her. I told them how I had reminded her that God expects *only faithfulness*, and that if she could tell me I had been faithful in lovingly caring for her, I knew God was pleased with me. That seemed to satisfy her, and she never expressed sorrow again over holding me back from preaching.

"Now," I said, "on this, the anniversary of her death (for she died one year ago tonight), I am sure there is nothing that would please her more than to know that I am in Japan, doing what I love to do, sharing with you dear Japanese people out of God's Holy Word."

I was amazed at the effect that statement had on the audience! Some were even weeping.

A missionary said to me after the service, "You have no idea how dramatic your final statements were! You couldn't know because you are unfamiliar with the Japanese culture. For them, the first anniversary of the death of a spouse is a *very* special day. Some will even hold a service of memorial, and all consider it a most significant day, almost sacred. It meant a lot to them to think that you had chosen to spend it with them!"

It meant a lot to me, too! God had deliberately transformed my difficult day into a happy anniversary!

Obliquely?

1995

_I_ had been doing better with handling grief for about ten days. Then a letter from my friend, Paul Bubna, triggered some pretty heart-wrenching sobs. Late into the night I typed my emotional response to him. I felt he understood me, for he had lost the darling of his heart just a week earlier than my loss of Elaine.

In my letter I was bemoaning the fact that there was not a soul on earth I could talk to who understood how deeply hurt I was. I went on to say, "God is real to me, and I can talk to Him, but He does not talk back much, except obliquely." I qualified that statement by recalling the "Happy Anniversary."

Somehow I think God was touched by my statement about His obliqueness and decided that He would "speak" so that I could hear His voice easily if I had a mind to. Rarely does God speak in a loud voice; He almost always speaks in a "gentle whisper." What follows tells you how He spoke on this occasion.

I had been away for more than a week visiting Shell Point Village in Florida. Ken Stumbo, one of my staff at Fairhaven, took me to see how much they had accomplished on the chalet I was to live in. As we walked together, he asked me, "Did you plant some bergamot near the chalet?"

I thought I knew what he was referring to and replied, "No, Ken, I didn't. They just came up naturally. I didn't recognize their leaves; almost pulled them up!"

But that was *not* what he was talking about! Before I tell you what he really was referring to, I must be sure you understand the preciousness and beauty of the bee balm (or bergamot) wildflower. It is not frequently found. In our 100 acres at Fairhaven we may have a half dozen or more patches of it, and I am always grateful to God for letting us enjoy it. Usually it is red, and it is often called "Red Bergamot" as if there were no other color. However, on rare occasions you will see some white, and even more rarely, some lavender.

We entered the Rhododendron Chalet via the door that opens onto the deck on the street side. Then Ken opened the door on the other side of my chalet where the little "Serenity Creek" flows past. He pointed to a couple of large rocks not fifteen feet from my door. Growing around them in a beautiful arrangement were three lovely clusters of Bergamot, red, white and lavender. The three were growing together as one fabulous wildflower bouquet. I feel sure the naturalist would say, "That is quite *unnatural*. It is the obvious product of human intervention."

That must have been why Ken was thinking that I had transplanted them. Since I didn't, Who did? (The capitalization of the "W" in that question is by design.) Can it be that those beautiful bee balm were planted by a Triune hand. And, as He was planting them, did He say to Himself, "Is my response to this child I love *really* oblique? I speak directly, when he's listening!"

A Drink of Water for Whom?

1996

The trip to Sri Lanka was a long one! My journey took me from Fort Myers to Orlando, then from Orlando to Atlanta, Atlanta to Zurich and finally Zurich to Colombo, Sri Lanka.

In Zurich I had three hours to wait for the flight to Colombo. I approached the counter to enquire about the gate from which it would be departing. A gracious man with an accent was in line ahead of me and I heard him enquire about flight 582 on Air Lanka to Colombo! I deliberately eavesdropped as the attendant gave him gate information. Then I commented to him that I was headed there, too. He was warm and immediately open to conversation. We asked to sit together on the plane and also found a seat together in the waiting area where we chatted.

He was Dr. Nalin Ranasinghe, a philosophy professor at a major Catholic university. As we talked I began to sense that this was "ripe fruit" the Lord had sent my way. There was a spiritual hunger, a responsiveness to truth. Before I knew he was Roman Catholic, when he had asked where I had studied, I had included in my "résumé" my experience of doing my practicum in counseling at the prestigious Loyola University (Catholic). God knew that would give us more common ground on which to base our conversation and our friendship.

Early in our conversations which spanned the next sixteen hours (three in the waiting room, two en route to Rome, two on the ground in Rome and nine in the air en route to Colombo) God chose to do something extraordinary! We were sitting in the waiting area in Zurich. As we talked, my mouth became more and more dry until I felt I could hardly keep my lips apart and my tongue off the roof of my mouth! I remarked to him that I was extremely dry-mouthed and thirsty, but that I was afraid to drink from the fountain there, as it might negatively affect my digestive system!

We talked a little more and suddenly I said, "Why, look!" Two seats away was a large container of bottled pure spring water, completely full. The safety seal had not been broken. The owner had apparently forgotten it.

"That must be providential!" Nalin remarked softly and pensively, as if in awe. He was deeply impressed.

I was deeply thankful. He would not accept any of it, as he felt God had sent it for me! I drank the entire bottle over the next hour, alleviating my somewhat dehydrated condition. The God who brought food to one of His servants, while in the line of duty as he sat by the brook Cherith, still provides for His own children in the most thoughtful ways.

More important to me was the fact that by doing it, God had obviously further opened the heart of a man whose heart was already searching for truth.

I know the drink of water was provided by the Lord, but a question remains in my delighted heart, *Was that done primarily for me, or was it done for Nalin's sake?* Probably for both, with the emphasis upon the latter. How much that is like the God I know and love to serve!

A Margaret?

1996

God does not view time the way we do. The Bible says that to Him a thousand years are like a day and a day is like a thousand years. That's a very interesting way of stating things! Both those statements are understandable by themselves, but together they appear to be a strange contradiction. Not so. With God, time does not have the same dimensions as it has with us.

In my grieving, I almost became convinced that the deep pain and loneliness would never go away. Sometimes it was as strong sixteen months after Elaine's death as it had been immediately after she died. One major compartment in my life was empty. When she had stepped up into the glorious consummation of her salvation, I had stepped down, in the deepest recesses of my spirit, into a heart-wrenching vacuum. As much of that vacuum as I was capable of permitting God to fill, He graciously filled with Himself.

But there were areas of my life that Elaine had so sweetly filled that were empty now. Some of my deepest feelings went unshared with anyone. The thing I most missed was a confidante to whom I could say absolutely anything without having to second-guess as to how it would be received.

Spiritually, God became more and more real to me. My ministry opportunities became wider and more frequent than they had ever been before. Yet my hours alone were often very lonely ones. I expressed my deep, heartfelt feelings through writing a book of devotionals entitled *From My Grieving Heart to Yours*.

The pain of my loss was intense for nearly two full years; the loneliness only seemed to deepen.

Then rather suddenly God lifted me up and out of that very dark valley of grief. The deep pain was gone. The hard crying was over. Why? What strange, inexplicable twist of emotion was this? Later I would realize that the deep grieving had lifted when I had completed the writing of the book on grieving. God chose to leave me in the extension to the valley of the shadow of death so that those devotionals could be more poignant, growing out of a current grief rather than from the memory of it.

Yes, the deep, almost unbearable pain was gone now, but the loneliness was not! So I hesitantly put a new item on my prayer list: "A Margaret?" The reason I used that name was because my dear friend, Don Trouten, had been so richly blessed with a most gracious new wife after losing his precious Elaine. Her name is Margaret. I wondered if God had a "Margaret" for me as well, since my own dear Elaine was gone from me forever (as far as this life is concerned).

It was very difficult for me to put that on my prayer list, and difficult also to pray the prayer. One day I expanded the prayer, saying to God, *Lord, if You do have a "Margaret" for me, it would be icing on the cake if she would be a retired missionary who has lived on a sub-*

sistence allowance all her life and does not have a lot to live on in retirement. The abundance You have so graciously given to me could be an extra special blessing to her. The lifetime health care I have already purchased for two persons at Shell Point Village could be Your way of providing for her.

One day I recalled a very special person I had dated forty-eight years earlier at the Missionary Training Institute (now Nyack College), when I was there preparing for the ministry. She was so lovely. She had dated me once, and then had refused a second date. That hurt my ego! Had I known the reason for her refusal that second time, I would have actually felt complimented! Her name was Colleen Johns.

There was a possibility of seeing Colleen again when I would go to Mahaffey Camp in Western Pennsylvania to minister some six months later. I just couldn't bring myself to write to her. That would come across as expressing an interest that I felt, but my love for Elaine made it seem like disloyalty or something similar. I could not fully analyze those feelings! Whatever happened would just have to happen naturally and not be forced. Colleen was a single missionary lady, now retired and living in Irvona, Pennsylvania.

When an invitation came for meetings in Ellisburg, Pennsylvania, I looked that up on the map and found it was located approximately three hours north of Irvona. If I went straight north, leaving the freeways in upper Virginia, and taking back roads, I would come to Ellisburg, passing within four miles of Irvona at Glen Hope! Irvona was where Elaine was born. I knew the very house in which she had been born. The amazing

thing was that Colleen, my date of forty-eight years earlier, had lived right across the street! I could make that
little detour and take pictures of Elaine's birthplace to
give to my sons, Brian and Gary. And perhaps I could
also see Colleen!

I wrote her a letter, telling her that my travels would
be bringing me right through Glen Hope, only four
miles from where my honey had been born, so I was
planning to come and take pictures. I asked her if she
would happen to be at home at that time, and if so,
would she consider going out to lunch with me, so we
could reminisce about Elaine, college days and things
like that.

I waited and waited and waited for an answer. None
came. Each passing day brought more painful discouragement to my heart. Why didn't she answer? She was
always such a poised, gracious, considerate person
back in college days. She would not treat me this way,
would she? Even if she still did not want to have a date
with me, she would at least gently turn me down with
a return letter! I felt confident of that. But I couldn't
deny the fact that day after day brought no answer.

I e-mailed my son Brian in Ecuador: "I just don't
like this 'teenage' business!" I complained. The roller
coaster of emotions was getting to me. At sixty-seven
years of age I didn't really want to go through the vi-
cissitudes of the dating game. Then, just five days before getting in my car to head for Irvona and Ellisburg,
I needed to compare a verse I was going to use for vesper service with the text in the Living Bible. I had not
used that paraphrase for a long time. There inside the
cover were two letters. One was the letter I had writ-

ten to Colleen! I had never mailed it! I had taken it to church with me, planning to swing by the post office afterward. Apparently I had forgotten to do that!

What should I do? I e-mailed Brian again, alerting him as to what had really happened and telling him I just couldn't get up the courage to make a phone call to her.

His response was terse and provocative! "Go for it, Dad! Give her a phone call!"

So, reluctantly, I decided to phone her. The first attempt produced a busy signal. An hour later her phone rang and rang and there was no answer. The third time I prayed, "Lord, if she does not answer this time, or the line is busy, I am not going to try again. If You are wanting me to see her, please let her answer."

She did!

When I asked her if I might stop by, she hesitated for a moment and my emotions took a big dip during that moment. Was I back to square one with her?! Then she explained. "We are having a family reunion next weekend to celebrate two birthdays, but you come anyway and have lunch with us!" She was actually warmly presenting the alternative plan.

I demurred, but she insisted. Her melodious voice brought back so many memories. The sweet girl who had turned me down was actually saying "Yes" this time! Maybe it did not represent an interest in me, but was just a way of letting me reminisce and express my grief. I didn't want to read more into it than I should. I didn't remember that she had not sent a sympathy card or letter when Elaine died. Had I realized, I would never have guessed the reason for that, either (any more than I had guessed why she had turned me down for a second date way back in Bible college days, forty-eight years earlier!).

I deliberately arrived the night before the noon rendezvous. I wanted to find the house, so I would not be late the next day. The pretty little Amish candle in each window of her home reminded me immediately of my plans to have one in each window of my Shell Point Village retirement apartment. I had even paid extra to be sure there would be an outlet directly beneath each window and had already purchased the electric candles.

I found a little rooming house in Coalport, two miles to the South. I stayed there that night. Across the street was a florist where I purchased a beautiful planter to give to the family for their celebration. I really wanted to give flowers to Colleen, but felt that was too forward. I asked the family members whose birthdays were being celebrated to just leave the planter for her when they went back home. They could hardly divide it, anyway. I paid extra to have daisies in water picks added to the planter to make it almost like a flower arrangement with lots of greens.

I was so very nervous when I pulled up to the house and knocked on the door! Colleen answered and received me most graciously. She alleviated my nervousness immediately. The family insisted that we go on out for lunch and leave them to fend for themselves. I didn't want them to do that but didn't argue too much. I guess the truth is that I *did* want them to do that!

We went to Sir Barney's restaurant, a few miles from her home. The three hours we spent together seemed to fly! We shared our more recent years when we had both been caregivers, admitting to each other that the heavy responsibilities had exacted a big emotional toll. How precious those hours were with someone who understood me so well, and who felt as if I could share her deepest feelings, too. I loved it!

Early on in our conversation she brought up the fact that she had not written to me or sent a sympathy card when Elaine passed away. Cautiously she explained that she had wanted to, but was concerned about the appropriateness of her making a contact at a time like that, since I had shown an interest in her back in Bible college days. She thought it might appear forward, or represent wrong motives. She had cared about my sorrow and prayed for me, though she had not felt free to express her sympathy.

Looking at my watch, I said with reluctance, "I am going to have to take you back home right now, or I won't 'get me to the church on time' to preach tonight!" Before leaving her home to drive on to Ellisburg, I got up my courage and asked, "Would it be all right if I were to stop on my way back through after these meetings are over, so we could go out for lunch together again?"

"I'd like that!" she replied readily.

Oh, how I clung to those four words in the half-week that followed while I ministered in Ellisburg! I had seen her only once, and my heart was already entwined, *seriously*! I knew it, though I kept trying halfheartedly to repress those feelings.

We spent five hours that second time, in the Arrowhead restaurant in Clearfield. Five wonderful hours that made me never want to leave her! Had I met my "Margaret"?

I still didn't know why she had turned me aside in Bible college days. That information would come later when I would learn that her policy was not to accept a second date with any fellow that she felt she could become interested in unless he obviously had the call of God, as she had, to the mission field. She was determined that no relationship, no matter how appealing, would derail her from God's call upon her life or from God's will for her life.

My call from God was crystal clear too, but it was to the pastorate. So she had to say "no" and was too much of a lady to tell me that it was because she liked me. To tell the truth, I didn't even need that information right now. My heart was resting on cloud nine, and my emotions were running far ahead of my sensibilities! I was scared by the thoughts I was thinking and would not let her know them until a few months later!

Should I do nothing about decorating my Shell Point Village apartment, so she could have most of the input?

Stop thinking that way! What is the matter with you?!

When could we marry that would be a convenient time for my dear family in Ecuador to be able to be present?

Stop that! Do you hear me? Stop that!!

I found it virtually impossible to get my heart to obey my mind, so I finally just gave in and fantasized to my heart's content! My "Margaret" more than likely was the one who lived in the cozy home directly across the street from the little house in which my sweetheart of forty-one years had been born!

How could God be so good to me? My heart was singing again, for the first time in a long, long time. I was climbing rapidly up and out of the valley of the shadow of death now, scrambling with eager steps toward the sunlight, glad to leave behind the heart-pain and the spirit-gloom and the ever present mists and the loneliness.

A lovely "Margaret," whom I had admired and courted forty-seven years earlier, had been returned to me. We would be able to enjoy together the delights of picking up right where we had left off nearly five decades earlier. How perfect is the planning of God! How long-range, too! His ways are past finding out.

My "Margaret" (Colleen) was to become the new joy of my life; a new person to whom I could give all the tenderness, loving care and expression of human devotion that God had created me to give. In my heart I knew it was right. In hers, the feelings were identical! The God who is love had shed abroad in our hearts a love that would grow and grow into a thing every bit as beautiful as the love that Elaine and I had felt for each other. This was not to be a competitive relationship. No, it had been designed by God to be beautifully complementary!

A Blockade Removed

1996

*I*rvona, Pennsylvania was 500 miles from Roan Mountain, Tennessee. How could we ever explore our relationship further in a meaningful way? Letters and telephone conversations would be poor substitutes for face-to-face encounters, particularly at this early stage of renewing our friendship.

I did have a week of vacation coming up in a lovely town house on Sanibel Island in Florida. I had written to the owners to be certain they had not let someone else have it for that week. I would be on my way to the island of Bonaire, stopping off in Fort Myers for a breather before going on to minister to the TransWorld Radio missionaries at their transmitter site off the coast of Venezuela.

Rosalys Tyler, one of my friends at Shell Point Village, knew that I was wanting to vacation on Sanibel, near Shell Point Village. A letter arrived from her telling me that Mary Zebley, a Shell Point Village resident, was going away for those very dates and she would be glad to let me stay in her lovely riverside apartment. If I were to stay in Mrs. Zebley's apartment, I would be right there on the Shell Point island near my friends, and not ten miles away on Sanibel. Her letter was followed the very next day by one from the Shanks telling me that their town house on Sanibel was indeed available to me.

I have two lovely places to stay, I thought. *What am I ever going to do with two? How will I choose which one?!* Suddenly I was struck with a most delightful prospect! *What if Colleen were to stay in Mrs. Zebley's apartment, and I in the one ten miles away on Sanibel? Could anyone judge us for that? We aren't kids anymore. If we were, I wouldn't even think of it. But we are not! No one could rightfully condemn us for that! Do I dare ask Colleen to consider it? Will she think me too forward? What shall I do?*

An echo seemed to reverberate from somewhere: "Go for it, Dad! Phone her!"

But will she think me too forward? Will she be frightened by my aggressiveness? Am I rushing things too much? Shall I follow my heart or my brain? What shall I do, Lord?

I went for it!

"Colleen, how would you like an all-expenses-paid vacation in Florida?" I asked. I told her about the availability of the apartment and about the frequent flyer miles I could use for her ticket.

"Give me a couple of days to think and pray about it," she suggested.

Certainly! (*But, oh please, say, "Yes!"* I didn't really say that, but it surely was in my mind!)

When I called her a couple of days later, she agreed to this arrangement, and I don't even think there is a cloud with the proper number on it to describe which one I found myself on! Prior to that week in Florida, we attended the General Council of The Christian and Missionary Alliance in Indianapolis, Indiana. We were together through most of the sessions, and we had confirmed to our hearts by so many dear friends what we were already coming to know—this renewed relationship was of God and was for the rest of our lives. We were elated!

Those days in Florida were precious. We walked together and talked together and ate our meals together and explored the Village together and had devotions together. What a week of togetherness! Before the week was over I asked Colleen if she would marry me.

She said, "Yes!"

God had arranged for us a solid week of getting to know one another better—well enough, in fact, to feel absolutely certain that He Himself had been the One who had brought us back together after a service-filled hiatus of forty-eight years. They were years during which Colleen had served the Lord faithfully as a missionary, and Elaine and I had served Him faithfully in the pastorate. God had found a way for us to eliminate the 500 miles between us and to spend quality time together where we could be assured over and over that this was His beautiful plan for us. He had used Mary Zebley and Lyle and Gail Shank to make two lovely places available to us in which to stay during our speeded-up "courtship." He cares about every detail of our lives. Every last detail. We must never forget that!

A Classy Restaurant

1996

The engagement ring was in my hand now, and I was eager to get it on hers. I knew I would be speaking at Mahaffey Bible Conference the week after procuring the ring in Canada. So I wrote to the Chamber of Commerce in each of the larger Western Pennsylvania towns in a radius of seventy-five miles of the conference grounds. Where in this section of Pennsylvania would I ever find the kind of restaurant I would like? My son Brian had given his fiancee her ring in a revolving restaurant at the top of a skyscraper. I thought that was very romantic. But where could I find something similar in coal country?

The Chambers of Commerce of Altoona, Clearfield, Holidaysburg and Tyrone were as helpful as they could be under the circumstances. But none of them had anything like a skyscraper, of course. Then I noticed another town on the map that was printed in a little darker print—Indiana!

I was startled! *So that is where Indiana, Pennsylvania is situated!* I thought to myself. *Why, I know the mayor of that town!* I sat down and wrote him a letter, describing what I was searching for.

In response, he phoned me! "It's all settled," he said with firm excitement. "You are to come to Indiana that night, and we will have 'reservations' for you in the classiest 'restaurant' you have ever visited!" (Actually, he gave me some of the details, which I kept secret from Colleen and will for now keep secret from you, as well.)

When the night itself came, we got dressed up and left Mahaffey Camp headed for our special night out. There was no way to surprise her with the ring, but at least the place itself could be a surprise. It took a while of noticing which way we were headed before she settled on Indiana as being our destination. I teased her with bits of information like, "I have really lost control of this evening, honey! It is totally out of my hands. I am not concerned about the food or the ambiance, but I am a little bit uncertain about the 'floor show' because I don't know what it will be like."

"Floor show!"

"Yes, but put those words in quotes," I cautioned. I also told her we would have to move right along in order to meet our escort at the edge of town.

"Escort? What kind of an escort?"

"Well, it could be a police cruiser, or it could even be the mayor of the town himself!"

She laughed, and I laughed with her. She *knew* I was just teasing!

When we pulled into the rendezvous location, a luxurious car pulled in right behind us with a handsome looking couple in it. They stepped out, and so did we and I said, "Honey, I would like to introduce you to the mayor of this city, the Honorable J.D. Varner, and to his wife, Daria!"

I wish you could have seen the look on her face. It was a look of incredulity. Yet she sensed I was not joking, but was telling the truth!

The mayor and his wife escorted us through their beautiful city (where Jimmy Stewart had lived), and on out to the other side. We went a few miles toward the next town and then turned right onto a paved road.

The mayor stopped his car and came back to our window. He pointed to a clearing on the top of the mountain where a beautiful, large chalet had been erected. "That's where we are headed!" he exclaimed.

Colleen and I were both very impressed, but she did not yet know the remarkable details of the evening ahead of us! We turned off onto an entry road and wound our way up until we were at the summit where "Highpointe" was perched, commanding a 180-degree view of the lush valley below and of the distant ridges.

"Welcome to Highpointe!" Mayor Varner said.

They took us inside and introduced us to their son, Doug, the personal waiter we were to have. He was formally dressed, including cummerbund and bow tie, with a towel over his arm—the epitome of elegance!

The chalet itself had large casement-type windows across the front of it, each looking out on that glorious view. In front of one of them in about the middle was a table set for a queen! Flowers, candlelight, elegant china and much silverware were all artistically placed. The table for two, smaller than a game table, was just right!

The mayor and his wife left us with our private waiter, private chef, whom he had also hired for the evening, and private violinist—the "floor show"! Our waiter took us up into the beautiful loft where hors d'oeuvres were awaiting us. There was a cheese ball, shaped into two hearts and resting on broad-leafed lettuce, with a variety of crackers and a dainty knife to spread the cheese.

In a silver cooler on a pedestal were two bottles of sparkling grape juice, both red and white. He asked our preferences and then poured the "wine" into our long-stemmed glasses, first placing a dainty linen napkin on our hand and then the wine glass. All was executed to perfection, as if this were his occupation! He said, "Enjoy! I will leave you now, and will announce to you when dinner is served."

We sat there close together in the loft, feeling as if we were dreaming. I took pictures on the one-time-use camera Mayor Varner and his wife had provided for us, to prove that this was not just a wild fantasy!

When Doug announced, "Dinner is served," we left the loft and were seated at the beautiful dinner table by the window. More pictures. Nancy Otto, the chef, outdid herself with a magnificent meal, each course served so beautifully and photographed by Doug. Steve Stokes, our personal musician, came in with his violin and began to play love songs, classical songs and hymns. That "floor show" would have pleased any Christian! It was simply elegant. The evening was perfect.

When I presented the ring to Colleen, Doug again took pictures, even of my placing the ring on her finger.

After the individual deep-dish peach pies had been served, the waiter cleared away the dishes and then all three of them left so we could be alone. The evening was as romantic and special as I could have ever ordered! Through the kind mayor of Indiana and his dear wife, Daria, God had arranged for a truly classy restaurant.

Engagement Sequel

1996

*I*n some ways what was to happen next would be even more dramatic than the beautiful evening itself. It would reveal the special arrangements God Himself makes, quite unassisted by human hands!

Colleen and I left Highpointe thrilled with the memories of that romantic evening. We drove slowly down the mountain, remarking that we had not realized how far we had climbed from the paved road. After turning right onto the side-road pavement and then left onto the main highway, we came to the outskirts of Indiana.

We stopped at a traffic light, and I noticed that the engine light was coming on intermittently. We started up the hill and suddenly lost all lights and engine power. The car stalled! Everything was dead. There was no power at all, not even for flasher emergency lights. The highway was only two lanes and I was worried that someone barreling down the highway might come upon us and crash into the back of our car, as there were nothing but weak reflectors to warn them.

We had prayer. I backed down the hill and into the parking lot of the Canterbury Commons, a large apartment complex. It was late and dark, and this was a climax to a beautiful evening that I did not want! Everything had been so perfect up to this point.

Then we heard a car starting. I stepped out quickly to flag the resident down before he exited the parking lot. He saw me and immediately stopped. What a special young man God sent to us! No one could have been nicer or more helpful. When he heard our story, he told me he knew of no car rental agencies open at that time of night nor even of a garage with an all-night mechanic. He suggested that I call the mayor and tell him of our predicament. I didn't want to, for he had already done so much for us, but Fred insisted. He even looked up the number and dialed it for me.

"We're in trouble!" I told the mayor. When he heard the nature of it, he said, "It's no trouble, you are going to continue right on with this beautiful evening. Just stay there and in ten minutes I will be there with a car for you to take back to Mahaffey. Tomorrow I will have the car towed and repaired, and will call you at Mahaffey when it is ready for you to come back to get it."

True to his word, in less than ten minutes, he was there. He brought with him a beautiful Oldsmobile Aurora. Wow! What a car! He insisted we use it.

As we drove on toward Mahaffey in luxury, I noticed that the clock on the dash was at ten minutes of 12. "Honey," I said, "we have a problem. We are thirty minutes from Mahaffey, and in just ten minutes this fabulous car is going to turn into a pumpkin!"

The next day I waited all day for the mayor to call, but he didn't. I felt increasingly uncomfortable about keeping his luxurious car, so I made arrangements for someone to follow me, when my speaking obligation was completed, so I could return the car to Indiana. I made phone calls to the mayor's office, then to his place of business and then to his home, but could not find him at any of those places!

I went down to the speaker's cottage to change into my "speaking clothes" and *there was the mayor!* He had brought Colleen's car, all fixed and ready to use! It was such a surprise to see him! When he told me he wanted to stay to hear me speak, I suggested that he might slip in by the back door of that large auditorium so Colleen would not see him. I told him I was reciting to the people all the wonderful things we had enjoyed the night before and then calling her up to the front. I wanted then to call the mayor up as well and surprise her again with his presence.

It all worked. They clapped loudly for her as she came up to join me, for she was one of their own cherished missionaries from that district. Then when I asked the mayor to join us, she gasped with surprise. They stood to their feet and gave him a standing ovation as he came down that long aisle. It was an exciting moment.

At that point I asked the mayor to say a word, and he related a personal experience that made goose bumps come out all over me. People were crying as he told it. It was recorded, so let me quote him directly from the tape:

> "I would be honored to share a few words. The first thing I want to tell Colleen is that I have a bill for $8,346."

> Everyone laughed, and Colleen responded, "You can have the car!"

> More laughter.

> "No, the car has been repaired, and it was just our privilege. I want to say to you briefly, I'm a Methodist like John Wesley. You know, John was

out working for the Lord, and then he realized that he had to allow the Lord to do a little work in him. I've been that sort of person myself, working for the Lord, and then realizing I had to allow God to do a little work in this life in order to set me free from the past and set me free for the future. And Dr. Charles Shepson has played a marvelous role in my life.

"A few years ago, after some thirty years in Christian ministry—I do a radio show in Indiana called 'The Christian Witness'—I found myself being unfaithful. One of the pitfalls in ministry is that when you have stumbled, the tendency is to try to protect the ministry by not confessing your sins. Who do you talk with when you are a Christian leader and have a problem? One of the great lessons I have learned from Dr. Shepson and others like him is that you have to learn to be honest with God.

"Having gone through the very difficult days of being discovered in my unfaithfulness, the only place I knew to go was Fairhaven Ministries. I called and made arrangements to go down there where I met a wonderful Christian counselor by the name of Ed Smelser. My heart was absolutely broken, my spirit was on the rocks. I didn't know if God would even look at me.

"It took me three days to get completely honest with God, and completely honest with my wife. On that third day, after confessing and breaking my wife's heart, I did a little penance. There is something in this human spirit that says, *Oh, God let me do something that will make it seem like I've done something to make it right!* So I started picking up garbage along Roaring Creek Road that runs through Fairhaven. Picking up litter, I thought, *Oh, God, how can anyone contaminate Your beautiful creation like this?* Then God began a Sunday school lesson with me. He said, 'Son, you have been contaminating My creation.'

"Then I found a license place, and I thought, *Now here's somebody who has been contaminating this beautiful countryside and this person is going to be held accountable.* God said, 'Son, I have your license number. I am holding you accountable.'

"Then, going down over the hill, I stumbled and fell, and that garbage bag burst open. The only way I could gather it together was to simply clutch it to my chest. God said, 'Garbage that you are, I am going to hold you close to my chest. I am not . . . I am *not* going to let you go!'

"When I got down that hill, I went to the bridge over Roaring Creek. Now this was in February. You know what cold water is like in February? This is icy water coming down off the mountain. I had a can of Pepsi in my pocket and the top of it had been covered over with mud from my fall. I took that can of Pepsi out of my pocket and went down by the bridge and stuck it into Roaring Creek, and it was *instantly* clean.

"*Oh, God! If I could be washed and clean like that!*

"Then the old hymn came to mind: 'What can wash away my sin? Nothing but the blood of Jesus!' God was having His way with me.

"Before long I knew what I needed to do. I am a man who has been baptized in a church. I have been rebaptized in the Jordan River. But I knew God had to do a work in me and I knew God wanted to rebaptize me, so I took off my jacket, my sweater, my hat and my boots, and I went down into that frigid Roaring Creek water in February, and God baptized me.

"When I came up out of that water, He told me He was going to do all things new for me. He was going to make my marriage new. He was going to make my ministry new. He was going to restore my family.

"It has been three and one-half years since that momentous occasion in my life, and God is continuing to open opportunities to me. This was an opportunity for me and my family to be in ministry to another Christian brother and sister."

The mayor's testimony powerfully affected the people gathered there in that large auditorium at Mahaffey. After the service someone came to me weeping and said, "The mayor's testimony meant so much to me! I too have failed, and to hear of his restoration and to see his transparency about what had happened has meant more to me than I can express."

Now I understood why the car broke down. There was no question in my mind but that the Lord had worked all of this together for the good of those who heard that stirring testimony by the mayor of the city of Indiana. That was not to be the end of the matter, however. A little over a week later there would be another sequel to the engagement story.

1996

A week passed. The memories of that wonderful evening were still crystal clear in my mind. So were those of the sequel with the mayor's powerful testimony.

I had been ministering for five days at another conference held at Northern Pines on Green Lake in Wisconsin. It was time to leave Northern Pines now and go on to the third back-to-back conference at Edinboro in Western Pennsylvania. Tom Warner, the head of Northern Pines, had kindly arranged for limousine service to the Milwaukee airport from the George Williams College where the conference was being held. The owner of the limousine service himself appeared! He had learned on his car phone as he headed for his office in Milwaukee that one of his eighty drivers had not shown up for work and had left him with no one to come to chauffeur me to the airport. I thought it strange that he placed my luggage and my carry-ons on the backseat of his car and opened the front door for me, but then I realized it was his personal car and the trunk was perhaps filled with other things.

I found it quite easy to carry on a conversation with him, but he was unresponsive to the slightest reference to spiritual things. *Lord Jesus, You can open closed doors, no matter how hard they have been slammed shut,*

I prayed. *Please make a way for me to witness to this man. I know You can do it. But how?*

He mentioned something about his "girlfriend." He was in his fifties, I would say. Someone called on the cellular phone. The conversation was brief as he told the person he had someone in the car and would call back later. Before he hung up, however, he wished the person a happy birthday and repeated that he would call back later.

I conjectured that it might be one of his children or perhaps a grandchild. I did not probe, of course. I just continued to wait for the answer to my prayer. I also put together a possible scenario. Perhaps this man was divorced and now had a new girlfriend. Perhaps it was the other way around. Perhaps he became involved with this girlfriend, and then his wife divorced him.

Then came the breakthrough. I said something about having spoken at a conference in Western Pennsylvania prior to my coming to Wisconsin. Now I was returning to speak at another conference near Erie, again in Western Pennsylvania. I thought he might ask the nature of my lectures, but God had other plans.

The limo driver asked where the first conference had been, and when I said "Mahaffey," to my surprise he knew exactly where that little out-of-the-way town was!

"I am from back that way myself," he said. "In fact, my mother still lives back there, in Indiana."

"Indiana!? Really?" I said. "I can hardly believe this. I must tell you a story about something that happened back there a little over a week ago." I related the whole story. When I got to the part about backing down into the parking lot of an apartment complex, I even added that I thought the name of it was Canterbury something or other.

"Canterbury Commons," he said. "My mother lives in one of those apartments!"

His mother lives in the Canterbury Commons! What great credibility that gave my story! I went on to complete it. When I told about the mayor's testimony, he was obviously moved and troubled.

As soon as I had finished the story, he changed the subject abruptly without comment. It was apparently too painful or threatening for him to want to discuss. I went on my way into the USAir counter marveling at the way the Lord had worked. I wondered if that man had been unfaithful to his wife, as well, and if God had been using this to prick his heart. I wondered if his mother was a praying woman, asking the Lord that very moment to let someone cross his path who could be used of God to make him think seriously. I wondered if he were bright enough to realize the staggering odds that were needed for his mother to be in the very town I was talking about, and for her to live in the very apartment complex into which I backed our disabled car. I did some mathematical calculations, factoring in the number of states from which he might have come to Wisconsin, and then taking a smaller number because many of them are smaller than Pennsylvania. I took into account the number of cities and towns there are in Pennsylvania (more than 1,300) and cut that back to 1,200 to be conservative. I then considered the number of streets and individual locales in Indiana where his mother might have lived; realizing that probably not more than fifty percent of the men his age have a mother still living. I then estimated, very conservatively, that it could be said there was only one chance in 120 million (120,000,000) that his mother would be currently living in the Canterbury Commons apartment complex, in Indiana, Pennsylvania. I want to hear "the rest of the story" someday. Perhaps I will in heaven. I'd love to meet him there and have him tell me that story in person!

* * * *

And what about the rest of *our* story? To date it is a "lived happily ever after" scenario! More than 300 very special friends came to celebrate our marriage on October 26, 1996 at First Alliance Church in Toccoa Falls, Georgia. We have been extremely happy and are so grateful to God for bringing us back together after forty-eight years!

We have been building worldwide memories together, ministering in widespread and exotic places, primarily to missionaries. Those ministries have taken us to Austria, Thailand, Uruguay, Ecuador, England, Lebanon, Syria, Jordan, Canada, Israel and many places right here in our own country. Our "home base" is the Shell Point Village Retirement Community in Ft. Myers, Florida.

To God be the glory for all the "quiet miracles" of the past and the present. He is the same eternally.

Other Books by
Charles W. Shepson

How to Know God's Will
A Heart for Imbabura (Book 6 of
The Jaffray Collection of Missonary Portraits)